ROADS
roads.porsche.com

COSTA A CANNELLE D33

INTRO

Eigentlich ist das CURVES-Universum genau wie die Welt: Neben den großen, epischen Reisen durch Länder und manchmal sogar halbe Kontinente haben wir auch eine (überhaupt nicht so) heimliche Freude an den kleinen Inseln, die als Kleinode im Meer warten. Dass nach den rasanten Ritten durch die Berge Siziliens und über die Kurvenstrecken Mallorcas nun also auch Korsika ein weiteres Mittelmeer-Ziel sein musste, liegt auf der Hand: Korsika ist nicht nur exzellent per Fähre erreichbar, sondern hat auch anspruchsvollste Fahrstrecken, sowie eine urwüchsige Naturschönheit zu bieten. Dachten wir zumindest. Ganz pragmatisch. Als wir noch in den Reisevorbereitungen mit dem Finger auf der Landkarte unterwegs waren. Wie atemberaubend schön, träumerisch tief und atmosphärisch dicht die Fahrt über diese faszinierende Insel dann aber wirklich war, verblüfft uns immer noch. Wir haben auf unserem CURVES-Streifzug durch die Welt ganz bestimmt schon ein außergewöhnliches Maß an Schönheit gesehen, aber Korsika hat sich in unserer Hitliste der kleinen, feinen Kurventouren mit Leichtigkeit auf den ersten Platz geschoben. Einfach so. Ohne Drama, Trommelwirbel und Tusch – einzig durch einen wunderbar authentischen Charakter, kaum zu beschreibenden Lost-Places-Charme und einen zu Tränen rührenden Händedruck voll unverstellter Ehrlichkeit. *„Soulful Driving“* – auf Korsika ist das Motto von CURVES zum Mantra geworden.

—

The CURVES universe is actually just like the world itself: in addition to the big, epic journeys through countries and sometimes even half a continent, we also have a (not so) secret soft spot for the small islands that await us like jewels in the sea. It is clear that after the fast rides through the mountains of Sicily and over the winding roads of Mallorca, Corsica was bound to be another Mediterranean destination: Corsica is not just highly accessible by ferry, but also has the most demanding routes to offer, as well as areas of unspoiled natural beauty. At least so we thought in our very pragmatic way when we were still following the map with our fingers in preparation for the trip. We are still amazed at how breathtakingly beautiful, profound and intense the journey across this fascinating island really was. We have certainly seen an extraordinary amount of beauty on our CURVES forays throughout the world, but Corsica has easily pushed itself into first place on our list of small, fine curve tours. That's the simple truth. No drama, drum rolls or fanfares – just a wonderfully authentic character. The island has an almost indescribable long-lost charm and an open handshake full of undisguised honesty that can move you to tears. *"Soulful Driving"* – the CURVES motto became our mantra on Corsica.

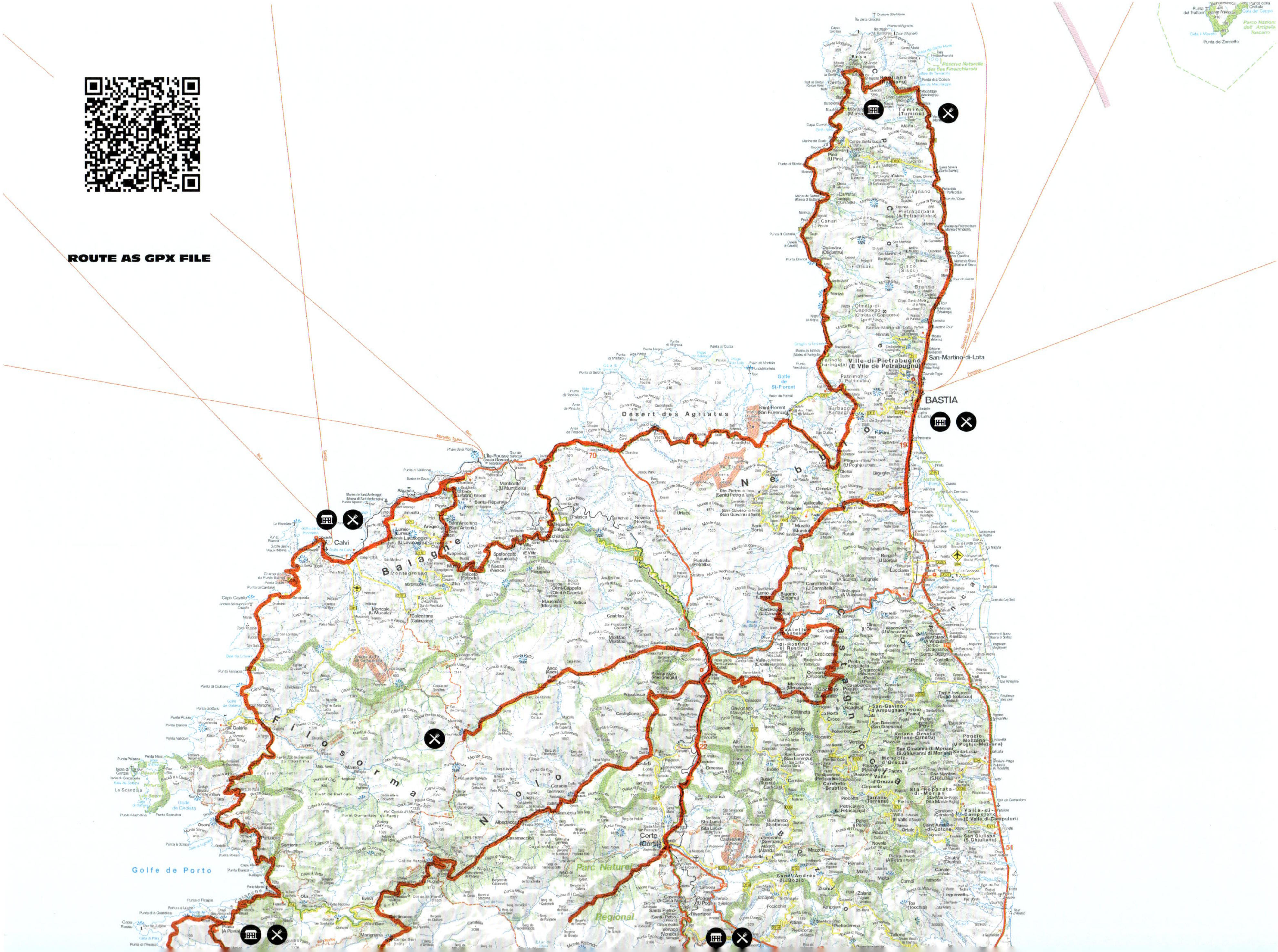

ROUTE AS GPX FILE

MER TYRRHÉNIENNE
MER DITERRANÉE
Golfe de Sagone
Golfe d'Ajaccio
Golfe de Valinco
Bouches de Bonifacio
AJACCIO (AIACCIU)
Porto-Vecchio (Portuvechju)
Sartène (Sarté)
Santa-Maria-Figaniella
Réserve Naturelle des Bouches de Bonifacio

PIANA D81

1 ETAPPE STAGE

Mit der knapp 50.000 Einwohner großen Hafenstadt Bastia beginnt unsere Reise rund um und über Korsika. Hier landen die meisten Fähren vom Festland, die italienischen Städte Genua, Livorno und Savona binden Korsika vom Norden und Osten her an, vom französischen Festland her bedienen Fährverbindungen aus Nizza, Toulon oder Marseille die Insel. Unsere Route führt uns von Bastia aus nach Norden, wir umrunden zuerst hauptsächlich auf herrlichen Küstenstraßen die nördliche Halbinsel des Cap Corse. Im Westen der Insel angekommen durchqueren wir die karge Désert des Agriates, eine nahezu baumlose Gegend mit ausgeprägt landwirtschaftlicher Tradition. Zwischen Küste und Bergen im Landesinneren stoßen wir dann in weitem Bogen in die Gegend rund um die Stadt Calvi vor, von hier aus führen besonders wilde Kurvenstraßen hinunter zum Golf von Porto, dem Ziel unserer ersten Etappe.

Our journey around Corsica begins with the port city of Bastia, population almost 50,000. Most ferries from the mainland dock here, the Italian cities of Genoa, Livorno and Savona connect Corsica from the north and east, while ferry services from Nice, Toulon or Marseille serve the island from mainland France. Our route takes us north from Bastia. We first circle the northern peninsula of Cap Corse, mainly on beautiful coastal roads. Arriving in the west of the island, we cross the arid Désert des Agriates, an almost treeless area with a strong agricultural tradition. Navigating between the coast and the mountains of the island's interior, we advance in a wide arc to the area around the city of Calvi, where particularly wild, winding roads lead down to the Gulf of Porto, the end of our first stage.

2 ETAPPE STAGE

Surf and Turf – das könnte als Motto der Etappe entlang der Westküste Korsikas taugen. Immer wieder zieht uns das Mittelmeer magisch an, wir entdecken die Schönheit unzähliger Buchten und Steilküsten. Die Streckenführung hält dabei meist einen topografisch bedingten Sicherheitsabstand ein, wilde Küstengebirge machen den direkten Zugang zum Meer unmöglich – und wunderschön. In bester Aussichtslage fahren wir vom Startpunkt am Golf von Porto auf steilen Klippen nach Süden und verschwinden dann immer wieder in den Bergen des Landesinneren. Erst rund um die Mündung des Flusses Liamone ist das Land flach, hinüber in die korsische Hauptstadt Ajaccio geht es dann aber wieder kurvig weiter. Mit einem Abstecher ins hochalpine Landesinnere setzen wir einen abenteuerlichen Akzent, über Propriano und Sartène geht es zurück an die Küste. Nach einem weiten Bogen um das Küstengebirge am „Punta Di Capuneru“ sowie den Meeresarm bei Figari landen wir in Bonifacio, hier haben wir die Südspitze Korsikas erreicht.

Surf and turf could be the motto of the stage that follows the west coast of Corsica. Again and again the Mediterranean attracts us magically, as we discover the beauty of countless bays and cliffs. Topographical features mean that the route usually keeps a safe distance, as wild coastal mountains make direct access to the sea impossible, but make up for this with their beauty. From our starting point on the Gulf of Porto, we head south on steep cliffs, enjoying the best panoramic position, and then disappear over and over again into the mountains of the interior of the country. The only flat part of the island is the area around the mouth of the Liamone River, which then becomes hilly again as we near the Corsican capital, Ajaccio.A detour into the high alpine interior of the country lends a touch of adventure to our journey as we return to the coast via Propriano and Sartène. After following a wide arc around the coastal mountains at "Punta Di Capuneru" and the estuary at Figari, we end up in Bonifacio at the southern tip of Corsica.

3 ETAPPE STAGE

Die Ostküste Korsikas ist deutlich ruhiger und weniger zerklüftet als der Westen, das Land ist flacher und die Strände breit. Was für Badeurlauber großen Reiz haben mag, ist auf der Suche nach Kurvenstraßen natürlich kein ideales Terrain. Auf unserer dritten Etappe verlassen wir die Küste daher zum ersten Mal für lange Zeit und fahren durchs Landesinnere des Südens der Insel. Beim kleinen Städtchen Zonza angekommen, legen wir aber trotzdem eine Schleife in Richtung des Meeres ein, verbinden die Fahrt über spektakuläre Bergstraßen mit einer kurzen Stippvisite an der Ostküste: Bei Porto-Vecchio sowie zwischen Favone und Solenzara weiter nördlich schnuppern wir ein letztes Mal Seeluft. Danach geht es im Solenzara-Tal und durch die nachgelagerten Canyons zurück nach Zonza, von hier aus weiter nach Aullène. Hier treffen wir auf ein Teilstück der Route unserer letzten Etappe, ab Zicavo sind wir aber wieder auf Neuland unterwegs. Über Cozzano geht es zur Grenze des Departements Haute-Corse und dann weiter ins Hochgebirge Korsikas. Am Etappenziel in Vivario haben wir die höchsten Berge Korsikas in Reichweite, so liegt beispielsweise der 2.389 Meter hohe Monte d'Oro auf dem Gebiet von Vivario.

The east coast of Corsica is much quieter and less rugged than the west, the land is flatter and the beaches are broad. Although this may be appealing to beach holidaymakers, it is, of course, not ideal terrain when you're looking for winding roads. On our third stage we therefore leave the coast for a long period for the first time and drive through the interior of the south of the island. Arriving at the small town of Zonza, we still make a loop in the direction of the sea, combining the drive over spectacular mountain roads with a short flying visit to the east coast: near Porto-Vecchio and between Favone and Solenzara further north we breathe in the salt sea air one last time. We then carry on to the Solenzara valley and through the canyons beyond back to Zonza and from there on to Aullène. Here we rejoin a section of the route from our previous stage, but once we reach Zicavo we are on terra nova once again. Passing though Cozzano we reach the border of the Departement of Haute-Corse and then move further into the high mountains of Corsica. The highest mountains in Corsica are within reach at our destination in Vivario, for example the 2,389 meter high Monte d'Oro is close by.

4 ETAPPE STAGE

In der Nordhälfte der Insel finden sich die höchsten Berge Korsikas. Hier sind wir auf der vierten Etappe unterwegs, fahren rund um den „Parc naturel régional de Corse" und bis hinauf an den Fuß des Monte Cinto-Massivs. Im kleinen Weiler Vivario mit seinen knapp 500 Einwohnern geht es los, in weitem Bogen südlich des knapp 2.390 Meter hohen Monte d'Oro vorbei. Auf halbem Weg in die Küstenstadt Ajaccio biegen wir dann nach Norden ab, bis nach Vico in der Region Cruzzini. Auf dem weiteren Weg südlich des Monte Cinto überqueren wir immer wieder kleine Straßenpässe, stoßen auf einer Art Kreisbewegung bis nach Castirla, einer kaum 200 Einwohner großen Gemeinde am Fluss Golo, zwischen dem Monte Pinerole (1.951 m) und Monte Agatu (1.641 m). Ziel der Fahrt ist Corte, ein Abstecher ins wunderschöne Restonica-Tal rundet die Route auf den Spuren der Korsika-Rallye ab.

The highest mountains in Corsica are located in the northern half of the island. Here we are on the fourth stage, driving around the "Parc naturel régional de Corse" and as far as the foot of the Monte Cinto massif. We start out from the small hamlet of Vivario, population almost 500, following a wide arc south of Monte d'Oro, almost 2,390 meters high. Halfway to the coastal town of Ajaccio we then head north all the way to Vico in the Cruzzini region. Continuing south of Monte Cinto, we repeatedly cross small mountain pass roads, taking a kind of circuitous route to Castirla, a community with barely 200 inhabitants on the river Golo, between Monte Pinerole (1,951 m) and Monte Agatu (1,641 m). The final destination of our trip is Corte, while a detour to the beautiful Restonica valley rounds off the route, following the route of the Corsica Rally.

5 ETAPPE STAGE

Zum Ziel der Reise in Bastia arbeiten wir uns durchs Gebirge nach Norden: Startend in der ehemaligen Hauptstadt Corte geht es über Castirla und Popolasca bis nach Ponte Leccia, hier fahren wir ins Tal des Asco hinein. Dieser Fluss speist sich aus dem Monte-Cinto-Massiv, sein Tal gehört zusammen mit dem Restonica-Tal weiter südlich zu den landschaftlichen Juwelen des korsischen Hochgebirges. Von der Mündung des Asco in den Gollo bis zum Ende des Tals im Hochgebirge fährt die Straße durch eine ständig wechselnde Landschaft, von beinahe mediterranem Ambiente bis in alpines Terrain. Mit einem Umweg über wilde Kurvenstraßen zwischen Morosaglia und Quercitello und dann weiter zur Abtei von Casablanca geht es in einem weiten Bogen nach Norden, über Campile landen wir schließlich an der Ponte Novu in Castello-di-Rostino. Auch bis nach Murato, Oletta und Barbeggio haben wir noch viele kurvenreiche Kilometer vor uns, erst danach geht es in entspannterem Gelände zurück an die Küste. In Bastia haben wir schließlich die Runde um und über Korsika geschlossen, die Fähre zum Festland wartet bereits.

We work our way north through the mountains to the final destination of our trip in Bastia: starting in the former capital of Corte, we pass through Castirla and Popolasca to Ponte Leccia, where we enter the Asco valley. This river flows from the Monte Cinto massif. Its valley, along with the Restonica valley further south, is one of the jewels of the Corsican high mountain landscape. From the point where the Asco flows into the Gollo to the end of the valley in the high mountains, the road bisects a constantly changing landscape, from an almost Mediterranean ambience to alpine terrain. Taking a detour via wild winding roads between Morosaglia and Quercitello and then on to the Abbey of Casablanca, we head north in a wide arc, via Campile and finally end up at the Ponte Novu in Castello-di-Rostino. We still have a long winding road ahead of us to Murato, Oletta and Barbeggio. Only then do we return to the coast and more relaxed terrain. In Bastia we finally complete the circuit around and over Corsica and the ferry to the mainland already awaits.

COL DE BAVELLA

EDITORIAL

Reinzoomen nach Korsika. Landeanflug aus dem All, immer näher kommen. Die über 2.000 Meter hohen Berge im Zentrum sind früh auszumachen, der lange Finger im Norden ebenfalls, schließlich werden auch die feineren Konturen der Insel immer schärfer: In weitem Bogen geschnittene Strände im Osten, eine gezackte und von unzähligen kleinen und großen Buchten durchwirkte Küste im Westen und Süden. „Immer im Westen", denkst du, „wie die Fjorde und Meeresarme in Norwegen oder Schottland – die Küsten im Westen sind gerne mal zerklüftet und turbulent, woran das wohl liegt?" – Dann wird der Blick wieder weiter, wir erfassen das ganze Bild. Korsika liegt als grüner Bergrücken im azurblauen Mittelmeer, 183 Kilometer lang und 83 Kilometer breit, leuchtende Wolken segeln über einen Sommerhimmel, weiß gischtende Wellen branden in endloser Stetigkeit gegen Felsen und Strände.

Nördlich von Sardinien liegt die Insel, südlich der italienischen Küste bei Genua, ungefähr auf Höhe der Toskana. Diese italienischen Referenzpunkte dürfen nun aber nicht darüber hinwegtäuschen, dass Korsika seit 1768 zum Staatsgebiet Frankreichs gehört – und da geht der Ärger schon los. Denn so richtig französisch wollten die Korsen nie sein, sehen sich als ganz eigenes Volk und dulden die französische Oberhoheit mehr, als sie wirklich zu mögen. Kein Wunder, schließlich mussten die Bewohner der Insel immer wieder erleben, wie sie von den unterschiedlichsten Festlands-Interessen als reine Macht-Manövriermasse benutzt wurden. Zuletzt eben Mitte des 18. Jahrhunderts, als die über Korsika herrschende Republik Genua die Unabhängigkeitsbestrebungen der Korsen in einem geschickten Schachzug zunichte machte: Nachdem auf Korsika die staatliche Unabhängigkeit samt einer demokratischen Verfassung ausgerufen wurde – zu diesem Zeitpunkt gab es eine solche nicht einmal in den USA – verkauften die Genueser Korsika 1768 einfach an Frankreich. Und die zu dieser Zeit im Powerplay der europäischen Supermächte militärisch gestählten Franzosen schlugen die Unabhängigkeits-

Imagine zooming in on Corsica from outer space. As we come closer and closer, the first things we see are the over 2,000-meter high mountains in the center, as well as the long finger of land in the north. Finally, the finer contours of the island come into sharp focus: the beaches in the east cut a wide arc, while the coastline to the south, east and west is jagged, interspersed with countless bays of varying sizes. "It's always the same in the west", you think, "like the fjords and inlets in Norway or Scotland – the coasts in the west tend to be rugged and turbulent, why is that?" – Then our view widens again and we take in the whole picture. Corsica forms a green mountain ridge in the azure Mediterranean Sea, 183 kilometers long and 83 kilometers wide. Luminous clouds sail across a summer sky, white foaming waves break endlessly against rocks and beaches.

Located north of Sardinia and south of the Italian coast near Genoa, the island is roughly level with Tuscany. However, these Italian reference points should not hide the fact that Corsica has been part of France since 1768 – and that's where the trouble begins. You see, the Corsicans never really wanted to be French. They regard themselves as a separate people and tolerate French rule rather than actually welcoming it. Small wonder. After all, the inhabitants found their island exploited over and over again by the most diverse mainland interests as a pawn in a power-based game. The most recent example was in the mid-18th century, when the Republic of Genoa, which ruled Corsica, destroyed the Corsicans' hopes of self-determination in a clever move: after state independence, including a democratic constitution, was proclaimed in Corsica in 1768 – at that time when such a constitution did not even exist in the USA – the Genoese simply sold Corsica to France. The French, militarily hardened by the power play of the European superpowers at that time, brutally crushed the independence movement in their new possession a year later. Since then, the Corsicans have been French citizens, but have never fully embraced that identity. The fact that Napoleon Buonaparte, born

Fantasien des neuen Besitzes ein knappes Jahr später kurzerhand blutig nieder.

Seitdem sind die Korsen französisch, haben sich aber niemals ganz mit dieser Identität angefreundet. Dass der 1769, also im Jahr der gewalttätigen französischen Annexion, im korsischen Ajaccio geborene Napoleone Buonaparte später einmal Kaiser Frankreichs und ein prägender Motor des französischen Imperialismus werden sollte, gehört wohl zu den überraschenden Wendungen europäischer Geschichte.

Korsika ist aber auch geologisch betrachtet das unstete Produkt äußerer Gewalteinwirkung, selbst wenn heute der äußere Eindruck das Gegenteil vermuten lässt: In den Flegeljahren unserer Erde, vor rund 35 Millionen Jahren, lag das, was heute Korsika ist, noch tief unter der Erdkruste verborgen. Als dann die afrikanische Platte von Süden dahertrieb und in einer Art Millionen-Jahre-Zeitlupen-Crash gegen die eurasische Platte trudelte, wurden nicht nur die Alpen zur sich aufbäumenden Knautschzone, sondern auch Korsika und das benachbarte Sardinien. Granit und Porphyr-Kristalle brachen in Form von Hunderte Meter hohen Gebirgsketten aus dem Boden, sie machen heute den Hauptteil der Landmasse Korsikas aus.

Im Osten der Insel falteten sich mürbe Schieferplatten wie Blätterteigschichten aus dem Grund früherer Urmeere empor, lediglich im Norden Korsikas findet sich weiches Schwemmland, das aus den späteren Jahrtausenden stammt. Damals ragte Korsika nach dem Erdkrusten-Crash als Gebirge aus einem trockenen Steppen-Trog, in dem riesige Tierherden grasten – dann entstand durch einen Durchbruch des Atlantiks an der heutigen Straße von Gibraltar binnen weniger Wochen das heutige Mittelmeer. Sintflut. Totale Apokalypse. Und Korsika wurde zur Insel. Von wegen, Geologie ist langweilig: auf Korsika ganz bestimmt nicht.

in Ajaccio in Corsica in 1769, the year of the violent French annexation, was later to become Emperor of France and a formative driving force of French imperialism is probably one of the more surprising twists of European history.

From a geological perspective, however, Corsica is also the unstable product of external forces, even if today's external impression suggests otherwise: when our earth was still in its infancy, around 35 million years ago, the place we now know as Corsica was still hidden deep under the earth's crust. When the African plate drifted up from the south and collided with the Eurasian plate in a kind of million-year slow-motion crash, the resulting buckling formed not only the Alps, but also Corsica and neighboring Sardinia. Granite and porphyry crystals erupted in the form of mountain ranges hundreds of meters high, making up most of Corsica's landmass today. In the east of the island, slabs of crumbly slate folded up like layers of puff pastry from the bottom of earlier primeval seas. Only in the north of Corsica is there soft alluvial land that dates back to later millennia. At that time, after the collapse of the earth's crust, Corsica rose as a mountain range from a dry steppe trough, where huge herds of animals grazed – then within a few weeks, today's Mediterranean Sea was formed when the Atlantic Ocean broke through at today's Straits of Gibraltar. The subsequent deluge brought total apocalypse and Corsica became an island. Who ever said geology was boring? It certainly isn't in Corsica.

But the Corsicans among our readers must now show great forbearance, because our voyage of discovery into the heart and soul of the island must now deal directly with the proud inhabitants themselves. If you look at things dispassionately, they only share one special characteristic: they are a colorful mix of descendants of travelers and settlers from all over the

Die Korsen unter den Lesern müssen jetzt aber ganz stark sein, denn auf unserer Erkundungstour in Herz und Seele der Insel landen wir nun direkt bei den stolzen Bewohnern. Und die haben, etwas herzlos betrachtet, nur eine Besonderheit: Sie sind bunt gemischte Nachfahren von Reisenden und Siedlern aus dem gesamten Mittelmeer-Raum. Genau wie die Mallorquiner, die Malteser, die Sizilianer, die Sarden ... Korsen haben ägyptisches Blut, karthagische DNA, griechische Vergangenheit, etruskische Seele, römisches Sein, sie sind germanische Vandalen, geprägt von Langobarden, Franken, Byzantinern, Toskanern, Genuesen – selbstverständlich haben sich sogar die Sarazenen auf Korsika verewigt. Und Hand aufs Herz: Selbstverständlich kennen die Korsen ihre Geschichte ganz genau. Nicht umsonst bekommt man nach ein, zwei Gläsern Pastis in den Hafenbars von Ajaccio oder Bastia vergnügt erzählt, es zeichne einen wahren Korsen aus, Berber-Blut zu haben, aber auch entfernte Verwandtschaft in Genua oder der Toskana und schließlich einen Onkel in der Pariser Verwaltung. So etwas wie „echte Korsen“ gibt es also nicht. Oder doch? – Denn vielleicht beweisen die Bewohner der Insel, dass nicht eine gemeinsame Herkunft oder Geschichte die wahre Klammer menschlicher Gesellschaften ist, sondern das Miteinander. Über Jahrhunderte hinweg hat sich im Druckkochtopf der abgeschiedenen Insellage eine ganz spezielle und eigene Identität entwickelt, in der selbst ehemalige Gegensätze oder sogar erbitterte Feindschaften Gemeinsamkeiten fanden.

Ein ausgeprägtes Wir-gegen-die-Welt-Gefühl mag eines der starken Merkmale Korsikas sein – und verständlich ist es allemal. Wer sich über Jahrhunderte hinweg konstant den Begehrlichkeiten und Übergriffen von kleinen Piraten und großen Imperien ausgesetzt sieht, entwickelt mit der Zeit eine Abstoßungsreaktion gegen äußere Ansprüche und Eingriffe, sammelt Trotz und Widerstandskraft und Eigensinn.

Mediterranean region. Just like the Mallorcans, the Maltese, the Sicilians, the Sardinians, etc., Corsicans have Egyptian blood, Carthaginian DNA, Greek heritage, Etruscan soul and Roman sensibilities. They are Germanic Vandals with influences from the Lombards, Franks, Byzantines, Tuscans, and Genoese. Of course even the Saracens had history in Corsica. Of course, the Corsicans know their history better than anyone. It is with good reason that, after a glass or two of pastis, in the harbor bars of Ajaccio or Bastia, you will be happily told that a true Corsican has Berber blood, but also distant relatives in Genoa or Tuscany and, finally, an uncle in the civil service in Paris. So there is no such thing as “real Corsicans”. Or is there? – It is possible that the inhabitants of the island will demonstrate that it is not a common origin or shared history that really holds human societies together, but rather a feeling of cohesion. Over the centuries, a very special and individual identity has developed in the pressure cooker of this isolated island community, where even former opponents or even bitter enemies have found common ground.

A distinct “us-against-the-world” feeling may be one of Corsica’s strongest characteristics, which is entirely understandable. Anyone who has been constantly exposed to the covetousness and encroachments of petty pirates and vast empires over the centuries will be repelled by external claims and interventions, building up a defiant, resilient and stubborn response. This is something common to islanders the world over. Their natural boundaries often become the perceived boundaries of the world for them. But what exactly is it that defines the inhabitants of Corsica? – You really shouldn’t judge that at all from the perspective of a mainland country, as the danger of stumbling into the pitfalls of prejudice and stereotypes is great. So we ask our sun-tanned heroes in the bars the same question – and are amazed by their answer.

Korsen haben ägyptisches Blut, karthagische DNA, griechische Vergangenheit, etruskische Seele, römisches Sein, sie sind germanische Vandalen, geprägt von Langobarden, Franken, Byzantinern, Toskanern, Genuesen – selbstverständlich haben sich sogar die Sarazenen auf Korsika verewigt.

Übrigens: Inselbewohner sind beinahe überall so, die natürlichen Grenzen werden bei ihnen nicht selten zu den gefühlten Grenzen der Welt. Was aber die Bewohner Korsikas ganz konkret ausmacht? – Das sollte man mit einer Festlands-Brille eigentlich überhaupt nicht beurteilen wollen, die Gefahr, ins Fettnäpfchen der Vorurteile und Stereotypen zu stolpern, ist groß. Fragen wir also wieder die sonnengegerbten Helden in den Bars – und staunen.

„Misstrauisch und schnell beleidigt", seien die Korsen, geben die Herren grinsend zu Protokoll, weshalb wir diese Eigencharakterisierung besser nicht allzu offensichtlich infrage stellen. Und lieber respektvoll nickend ein weiteres Glas Pastis stürzen.

Diese Zurückhaltung kommt anscheinend gut an, denn jetzt überbieten sich unsere korsischen Gastgeber mit knorrigen Attributen: „Mutig, gelassen und treu, gastfreundlich und erfrischend temperamentvoll" seien die Bewohner Korsikas, und wir können nicht anders, als diese Umschreibungen gegen die des griechischen Geografen Sabo zu stellen, der von den Sklavenmärkten der Antike berichtete und die gefangenen Korsen als besonders wild und trotzig beschrieb: Die auf Korsika Gefangenen hätten oft lieber Selbstmord verübt als in die Sklaverei zu gehen. Und der römische Schreiber Seneca weiß lakonisch zu berichten, der Kauf korsischer Sklaven lohne sich nicht, da die so unzähmbar starrsinnig seien ...

Eine weitere Diskussion lassen wir dann aus. Denn angekommen im Hier und Jetzt Korsikas, auf dieser saftigen, herben, schroffen, wilden Insel, schalten wir lieber um, von Verstehen auf Erfühlen. Vertrauen uns dem Flow der Reise an, treiben durch die intensive Schönheit der Berge, gehen hemmungslos verloren. Gelassen und mutig. Korsika macht eben selbst seine Besucher zu Korsaren.

Corsicans have Egyptian blood, Carthaginian DNA, Greek heritage, Etruscan soul and Roman sensibilities. They are Germanic Vandals with influences from the Lombards, Franks, Byzantines, Tuscans, and Genoese. Of course even the Saracens had history in Corsica.

The gentlemen tell us with a grin that Corsicans are "suspicious and easily offended". It's probably best not to question this self-characterization too closely. Instead we pour another glass of pastis with a respectful nod.

This reticence seems to go down well, because our Corsican hosts now outdo each other with gnarly attributes, telling us the island's inhabitants are "brave, relaxed and loyal, hospitable and refreshingly spirited". We cannot help but compare these descriptions with those of the Greek geographer Sabo who reported on the slave markets of antiquity and described the enslaved Corsicans as particularly wild and defiant: prisoners from Corsica would often have preferred suicide to slavery. Roman writer Seneca also reported laconically that buying Corsican slaves was not worthwhile because they are so untamable and stubborn.

We'll skip any further discussion because once we have arrived in the here and now of Corsica, on this lush, harsh, rugged, wild island, we'd prefer to depend on emotion rather than intellect. Entrusting ourselves to the flow of our journey, we drift through the intense beauty of the mountains, allowing ourselves to get lost without a second thought. Calm and courageous. Corsica turns even its most unassuming visitors into swashbuckling corsairs.

CANYON DE LA RUDA D84

PUNTA CODA D81B

COL DE BAVELLA

PLAGE DE NEGRO D80

OTA / EVISA D124

CALVI D81B

PIANA D81

GORGE DE L'ASCO D147

TRAGHINO D81

PIANA D81

PLAGE D'ALBO D80

MARIGNANA D84

D84

BASTIA
PORTO OTA

337 KM • 6 STUNDEN // 210 MILES • 6 HOURS

Ein knallbuntes Ungetüm wühlt sich mit prall gefülltem Bauch durchs Mittelmeer, pflügt eine Schleppe aus Schaum und Gischt in dunkelblaues Wasser. Möwen surfen Hang Loose in den unsichtbaren Wirbelschleppen, die riesige Schiffsaufbauten in Fahrtwind und Seewind fressen.

—

A brightly colored monster with a bulging belly plows its way through the Mediterranean, carving a train of foam and spray into the dark blue waters. Seagulls surf the invisible wake created by the huge ship's hull in the headwind and sea breeze.

HOTEL & RESTAURANT

PALAZZU NICROSI
LIEU-DIT VIGNALE
20247 ROGLIANO
WWW.PALAZZU-NICROSI.COM

LA VELA D'ORO
5193 MACINAGGIO
20247 ROGLIANO
TEL: +33495354246

Entspannt schmiegen sich Vögel in die strudelnden Strömungen der Luft, leuchten weiß am azurblauen Himmel, drehen Köpfe mit gelben Schnäbeln und patrouillieren in unregelmäßigen Pulks entlang des Schiffs. Die Decks aus Stahl vibrieren im gleichmäßigen Stöhnen mächtiger Dieselmotoren, gelangweilte Passagiere schlendern durch die immer etwas unterkühlten Gänge des Schiffs, warten auf die Ankunft.

Fünf Stunden dauert die Fährfahrt zwischen Genua und Bastia – eigentlich keine allzu lange Dauer. Vielleicht ist es ja aber das Gefühl von nicht diskutierbarem Ausgeliefertsein, das Fährüberfahrten so träge erscheinen lässt. Als sei man versehentlich in die Schleife eines Paralleluniversums gerutscht, die nun zu Ende gefahren werden muss, ob man will oder nicht. Um auf die Insel zu gelangen, muss man eben einen alternativlosen Weg durchs Nichts des Meeres zurücklegen und nimmt diese Erfahrung immer mit. Insulaner sind Menschen, die wissen, dass die Welt nicht rund und infinit ist, sondern dass sie ganz zweifelsfrei ein Ende hat. Beim Sinnieren über Inseln flackert dann für einen kurzen Moment dieser eine, abstruse Gedanke durch unseren Kopf, gerade wie die Halbnackten, die vor Fußballspielen über den Rasen des Stadions flitzen, bevor sie von der Security zu Boden gebracht werden: Ist womöglich Korsika das eigentliche Festland? Und tatsächlich der Rest der Welt die wahre Insel? – Vergnügt grinsend schaust du dieser Vorstellung nach, wie sie übers Spielfeld deines Gehirns hüpft, und bist beinahe enttäuscht, als sie von Ratio und Verstand festgesetzt wird.

Irgendwann taucht Korsika aus dem Dunst auf, ziert sich dann gefühlt endlos lang, wird einfach nicht größer. Die Uhr am Handgelenk läuft sinnlos vor sich hin, zählt bedeutungslose Sekunden, Minuten, beinahe Stunden herunter, ohne dass da vorn aus einer Ahnung von festem Land im Meer handfeste Realität wird. Die Propeller des Schiffs schäumen zornig vor sich hin, zig-

Relaxed birds find refuge on board from the buffeting currents of the air, glowing white in the azure sky, turning their yellow-beaked heads as they patrol the deck of the ship in irregular flocks. The steel decks vibrate with the steady chug of powerful diesel engines as bored passengers wander the ship's chilly corridors, impatient for arrival.

Taking about five hours, the ferry trip between Genoa and Bastia is not all that long. Perhaps it is the feeling of being at the mercy of something ineffable that makes ferry crossings seem so slow. It seems as if you have accidentally slipped into a loop in a parallel universe that now has to be completed whether you like it or not. In order to reach the island, there is no alternative except to traverse the nothingness of the sea, absorbing the experience for an eternity. Island dwellers are people who know that the world is not round and infinite, certain that it has its boundaries. As we ponder islands, an abstruse thought flickers through our heads for a brief moment, like a streaker who darts across the pitch before a football match only to be tackled to the ground by security staff: Is it possible that Corsica is really the mainland and the rest of the world the real island? – You grin happily as you watch this idea hop and skip across the playing field of your mind and are almost disappointed when it is caught by understanding and reason.

At some point Corsica emerges from the haze, then, for what feels like an age, just doesn't get any bigger. The watch on my wrist ticks away pointlessly, counting down meaningless seconds, minutes, almost hours, without any sign of solid land becoming a tangible reality up ahead. The ship's powerful propellers churn furiously, their tens of thousands of horsepower displacing the Mediterranean waters without any discernible effect. And then, suddenly, the island drifts towards us. It gets bigger and bigger, becoming clearer and clearer until, in the end, the ship emerges

D80

D80

tausend PS quirlen furios das Mittelmeer um – ohne irgendeinen erkennbaren Effekt. Und dann, plötzlich, driftet die Insel doch auf uns zu. Wird groß und größer, klar und klarer, am Ende zieht das Schiff als Sieger des Kampfes mit Raum und Zeit stolz durch die immer heller und flacher werdenden Gewässer rund um die Insel. Ein buntes Parkhaus aus Stahl im Meer. Drüben am Ufer steigt die Felsenküste Korsikas aus dem Wasser, türmt sich mit struppigem Grün bewachsen in die Vertikale. Am Fuß der Klippen ist eine kleine Straße zu erkennen, die hier entlang der Küstenlinie dahinwimmelt – sie werden wir nachher nehmen. Gespannt schauen wir hinüber, grüßen andächtig und folgen dem Verlauf der Straße mit den Augen.

Und dann schwenkt das Schiff nach rechts, zielt entschlossen auf die Kaimauern des Hafens von Bastia zu. Der öffnet ein gefräßiges Maul, saugt die Fähre an und schickt sie zur Verdauung auf einen Liegeplatz. Der Pott will nicht so recht, wehrt sich schäumend und mahlend gegen die Anziehungskraft des Landes und muss am Ende doch klein beigeben. Wird von mächtigen Tauen gegen den Kai gezerrt, an die Leine gelegt. Nun liegt er da, besinnt sich seiner eigentlichen Aufgabe und erbricht ganze Fluten von Menschen, Autos, Lkw, Motorrädern und Wohnmobilen auf das Hafengelände.

Der auf seinem Sockel in der Mitte des benachbarten Place Saint Nicolas stehende Marmor-Napoleon schaut dem Treiben entsetzt zu, irgendwie scheint er sich auch nach Jahrzehnten auf diesem Ausguck immer noch nicht an den Anblick der bei Ankunft von Schiffen ausbrechenden Hektik gewöhnt zu haben. Oder er befürchtet eben doch insgeheim den Verlust der Stola, die ihm sein Bildhauer in künstlerischer Freiheit etwas zu lose umgehängt hat. Wer weiß es schon? Statuen haben – so erzählt man sich – ein komplexes Seelenleben. Zu Lebzeiten eher klein gewachsene Diktator-Imperatoren machen da bestimmt keine Ausnahme.

Gespannt warten wir auf einen knappen Willkommensgruß, Herr Buonaparte scheint jedoch immer noch wegen Waterloo beleidigt zu sein, er schaut starren Auges aufs blaue Meer hinaus. Die schnurgerade gepflanzten Reihen von Palmen und Platanen rund um den Platz Saint Nicolas wedeln uns aber ein ebenso deutliches wie gelassenes Willkommen zu, und das lassen wir gelten. Wühlen uns mit dem Pulk der anderen Ankömmlinge vom Hafengelände auf die Hauptstraße hinaus und zuckeln geduldig so lange nach Norden, bis die Mehrzahl unserer Mitreisenden in den Gassen der Stadt verschwunden ist. Die letzten Ausläufer der automobilen Welle lassen wir dann nach ein paar Kurven ziehen: Bei einem kurzen Stopp tanken wir Sprit und Kaffee, rücken Landkarte und Sonnenbrille zurecht, lassen die innere Reise-Ameise warmlaufen. Jetzt geht es los. Korsika, wir kommen.

victorious in the battle with space and time and proudly cuts through the increasingly brighter and shallower waters around the island. The vessel looks like a colorful steel parking garage floating at sea.

Over on the shore, the rocky coastline of Corsica rises out of the water, towering above us, overgrown with scrubby vegetation. At the foot of the cliffs you can see a small road that weaves its way along the shoreline. We shall take it later. We watch excitedly, greeting the sights with due respect and following the course of the road with our eyes. Then the ship veers to the right, heading resolutely toward the quayside of the port of Bastia. The harbor opens like a voracious mouth, sucking in the ferry and dispatching it to a berth for digestion. The boat doesn't really want to cooperate, frothing and grinding as it resists the attractive force of the country before finally giving it. It is drawn up against the harbor wall by strong ropes, tamed on a leash. Now at rest, it returns to its actual task, disgorging hordes of people, cars, trucks, motorcycles and mobile homes onto dry land.

The marble statue of Napoleon standing on its plinth in the middle of neighboring Place Saint Nicolas surveys the hustle and bustle in horror. Somehow, even after decades on this perch, he still doesn't seem accustomed to the hectic eruption that breaks out every time a ship arrives. Perhaps he secretly fears losing the imperial stole that the sculptor, in an exercise of artistic license, has hung a little too loosely around his neck. Who knows? It is said that statues have a complex inner life. Short-statured imperial dictators are certainly no exception.

We eagerly await a brief welcome, but M. Buonaparte still seems offended by the outcome of Waterloo and continues to stare out at the blue sea, his eyes wide open. The straight rows of palms and plane trees planted around Saint Nicolas Square wave a welcome that is as clear as it is relaxed, and we are happy to accept that. We follow the throng of other arrivals from the port area onto the main street and patiently trundle north until the majority of our fellow travelers have disappeared into the city's narrow alleyways. After a few more curves, the last of the automotive wave passes: during a short stop we fill up on gas and coffee, unfold our map and straighten our sunglasses, and flex our travel muscles. Then, we're off. Corsica, here we come.

Gathering speed as we move away from the city, we first thread our way through the outskirts of Bastia. Motor scooters flash past, restaurants and cafés exude the aroma of fried food, children with unicorn swim rings scamper across zebra crossings to the small seaside bathing spots. The houses of the city begin to thin out and a few last party clubs and luxury resorts vie for attention with garish colors or an ostentatious display of a casual lack of ostentation –

D80

PLAGE DE PORTO NEGRO D80

FLNC

D81 / D38

D38

In versammeltem Stadt-Auswärts-Tempo schnüren wir zuerst durch die Randgebiete Bastias. Motorroller stürmen dahin, Restaurants und Cafés atmen den Duft von Frittiertem aus, Kinder mit umgelegten Einhorn-Schwimmringen flip-floppen über Zebrastreifen zu den kleinen Badebuchten am Meer. Die Häuser der Stadt verebben, ein paar letzte Party-Clubs und Luxus-Resorts heischen drall-bunt oder mit aufdringlicher Unaufdringlichkeit um Aufmerksamkeit – dann ist Schluss. Nur ein warmer Wind aus den mit Macchia bedeckten Steilhängen ist geblieben. Treibt uns voran, befeuert Lebens- und Reiselust. Kilometer um Kilometer geben wir uns diesem unwiderstehlichen Vorwärtsdrang hin, entdecken das altbekannte Phänomen „Küstenstraße" wieder einmal völlig neu. Fahren mit geblähten Nüstern, in die Sonne blinzelnden Augen und sanften Lenkbewegungen. Surfen nicht auf, sondern am Meer. Durch Kurven und Kehren, die sich in wilde Hänge schmiegen, während unter uns Licht auf Myriaden von Wellen glitzert.

In Macinaggio beendet die Straße selbst diesen Rausch: Sie zwingt uns in die Berge hinauf, kämpft wild mit dem harten Terrain und schwingt in vertrackten Moves durch diese nördlichen Ausläufer des Gebirges im Meer, das man Korsika nennt. Hinter dem kleinen Col Saint-Nicolas fällt das Gelände ab, schubst die Straße über die kleinen Weiler Baragogna und Mucchieta wieder ans Meer im Westen hinunter. Eine sprachlos machende Cinemascope-Landschaft breitet sich hier aus: Brachial ins weit unten liegende Meer hinunterstürzende Felsen, unnatürlich blaues Wasser, das an den Felssockeln von der schieren Wucht des offenen Meeres zu cremigem Schaum geschlagen wird, der dort unten dann auf rauem Granit gerinnt.

Kleine Dörfer und Kapellen krallen sich in die Hänge, behaupten einen Raum im Wildwuchs der krautigen, verbuschten, wilden Berge. Wir stranden vor einer der Bars an der staubigen Durchgangsstraße und schlüpfen hoffnungsfroh auf die Garten-Terrasse. Nicht lange danach bedecken Teller den Tisch, auf denen Zwiebeln und Fisch und gegrillte Fleischspieße und Gemüse in Olivenöl baden. Wasserperlen rinnen über eiskalte Gläser, ein warmer

then it's all over. All that remains is a warm wind from the steep, shrub-covered slopes. This drives us forward, fueling a love of life and travel. As we cover kilometer after kilometer, we surrender to this irresistible urge to move forward, rediscovering the familiar phenomenon of the "coastal road" in a completely new way. Our nostrils flared and our eyes squinting into the sun, we drive on with gentle, steering movements. We're surfing by the sea, not on it. We negotiate the bends and turns of the wild hillsides, while below us sunlight glitters on myriad waves.

The road itself brings this frenzy to an end in Macinaggio: it forces us up into the mountains, battling wildly with the harsh terrain and winding in intricate patterns through the northern foothills of the mountain range in the middle of the sea that we call Corsica. Behind tiny Col Saint-Nicolas, the ground drops away, pushing the road back down to the sea in the west through the small hamlets of Baragogna and Mucchieta. The landscape takes on a cinemascope dimension that leaves you speechless: rocks fall violently to the sea far below, unnaturally blue water is beaten into creamy foam by the sheer force of the open sea on the rock bases and then dries on the rough granite below. Small villages and chapels cling to the slopes, staking a claim to some space in the wild growth of the verdant, bushy mountain wilderness. We come to a stop in front of one of the bars dotted along the dusty thoroughfare and slip hopefully onto the garden terrace. Not long after, our table is groaning with plates of onions and fish and grilled skewers of meat and vegetables bathed in olive oil. Beads of moisture trickle down ice-cold glasses, a warm sea breeze causes the awning to flutter lazily above our heads. Perfection.

At this point we are definitely in the thrall of the wanderlust that has kept us on the move for as long as we can remember, causing us to stray with wide-open eyes, taking pleasure in the beauty of the big and small things in this world. – Already deeply in the flow, we continue to move onward and have soon reached the bay of Saint-Florent at the foot of Cap Corse, the finger-like peninsula in northern Corsica. While our journey

BAR
LICCIOLA
ROUTE DE BASTIA
LIEU DIT LICCIOLA
20226 PALASCA

D81

D38

D63

D63

CALVI D81B

HOTEL & RESTAURANT

HOTEL LA SIGNORIA CALVI
ROUTE DE LA FORÊT BONIFATO
20260 CALVI
WWW.HOTEL-LA-SIGNORIA.COM

LA CABANE DU PÊCHEUR
ROUTE DE BORD DE MER
20245 GALÉRIA

D81B

TRAGHINO D81

Links, rechts, links, rechts, hetzt sie atemlos dahin, in hartem Slalom. Bis Oletta, dann in einer Kehrtwende nach Norden bei Piève und ab hier in weitem Bogen durchs Gebirge bis kurz vor Ogliastro. Dass hier die Schnellstraße ans Meer unsere Route kreuzt, ist keine echte Versuchung, wenige Meter später geht es auch schon wieder ins Kurvengetümmel nach Novella.

Twisting left, right, left, right, it races along breathlessly, in a dizzying slalom. We reach Oletta, then make a sharp U-turn to the north at Piève and from here negotiate a wide arc through the mountains to just before Ogliastro. The fact that the expressway to the sea crosses our path here does not really pose any temptation and a few meters later we find ourselves back on tumultuous bends, heading toward Novella.

Seewind lässt die Markise über unseren Köpfen träge flattern. Perfektion sieht genau so aus. Und spätestens jetzt sind wir wieder in jenem Sog der Fahrt gelandet, der uns seit wir denken können auf die Straße holt, mit weit offenen Augen dahinstreunen lässt, voller Freude an Schönheit, den großen und kleinen Dingen dieser Welt. – Tief im Flow rollen wir weiter, haben auf Höhe der Bucht von Saint-Florent bald schon die Wurzel des Cap Corse erreicht, der fingerartigen Halbinsel im Norden Korsikas. Und während die Fahrt bisher den sanften Groove der Küstenstraße hatte, werden jetzt scharf gewetzte Kurven-Messer zwischen die Zähne geklemmt: Turbulent und derbe rockt die D38 ins Landesinnere, gönnt sich keinen Moment der Ruhe, keine Gerade. Links, rechts, links, rechts, hetzt sie atemlos dahin, in hartem Slalom. Bis Oletta, dann in einer Kehrtwende nach Norden bei Piève und ab hier in weitem Bogen durchs Gebirge bis kurz vor Ogliastro. Dass hier die Schnellstraße ans Meer unsere Route kreuzt, ist keine echte Versuchung, wenige Meter später geht es auch schon wieder ins Kurvengetümmel nach Novella. Ein paar weite Bögen später swingt die Straße in etwas gelassenerem Rhythmus, kreuzt auf Toccone zu, passiert Palasca und rackert sich dann viele Kilometer weit auf unstetem Kurs langsam auf die Küste bei Algajola zu.

Eine Bucht später haben wir mit Calvi zum ersten Mal seit Bastia eine etwas größere Stadt erreicht, lassen den Kulturschock der Autos, Einkaufszentren und mehrspurigen Straßen allerdings schnell wieder hinter uns. Bis zur Bucht von Crovani folgen wir noch in zurückhaltender Gangart der Küstenlinie, dann folgt in den Bergen hinunter zum Golf von Porto die absolute Kurven-Eskalation. Radikaler Kehren- und Serpentinen-Wildwuchs, völlige Abwesenheit jedweder Geraden, hemmungsloses Schwindligfahren. Korsika und wir, das ist der Beginn einer großen Freundschaft.

previously followed the gentle groove of the coastal road, a series of sharp corner are now to be negotiated with gritted teeth: head-strong and rough, the D38 turns inland, not allowing itself a moment's rest, not a single straight line. Twisting left, right, left, right, it races along breathlessly, in a dizzying slalom. We reach Oletta, then make a sharp U-turn to the north at Piève and from here negotiate a wide arc through the mountains to just before Ogliastro. The fact that the expressway to the sea crosses our path here does not really pose any temptation and a few meters later we find ourselves back on tumultuous bends, heading toward Novella. A few wide bends later, the road swings in a somewhat more relaxed rhythm, crossing toward Toccone, passing Palasca and then slowly toiling for many kilometers on an unsteady course toward the coast near Algajola.

After one more bay at Calvi, we have reached a somewhat larger town for the first time since Bastia, but quickly leave the culture shock of cars, shopping centers and multilane highways behind us. We follow the coast line at a modest pace as far as the Bay of Crovani, after which a tight series of curves takes us through the mountains and down to the Gulf of Porto. We navigate head-spinning hairpin bends and serpentines without a single straight section. It's just Corsica and us. This is the start of a beautiful friendship.

HOTEL & RESTAURANT

LES ROCHES ROUGES
ROUTE DE PORTO
20115 PIANA
WWW.LESROCHESROUGES.COM

BASTIA PORTO OTA

Mit der knapp 50.000 Einwohner großen Hafenstadt Bastia beginnt unsere Reise rund um und über Korsika. Hier landen die meisten Fähren vom Festland, die italienischen Städte Genua, Livorno und Savona binden Korsika vom Norden und Osten her an, vom französischen Festland her bedienen Fährverbindungen aus Nizza, Toulon oder Marseille die Insel. Unsere Route führt uns von Bastia aus nach Norden, wir umrunden zuerst hauptsächlich auf herrlichen Küstenstraßen die nördliche Halbinsel des Cap Corse. Im Westen der Insel angekommen durchqueren wir die karge Désert des Agriates, eine nahezu baumlose Gegend mit ausgeprägt landwirtschaftlicher Tradition. Zwischen Küste und Bergen im Landesinneren stoßen wir dann in weitem Bogen in die Gegend rund um die Stadt Calvi vor, von hier aus führen besonders wilde Kurvenstraßen hinunter zum Golf von Porto, dem Ziel unserer ersten Etappe.

—

Our journey around Corsica begins with the port city of Bastia, population almost 50,000. Most ferries from the mainland dock here, the Italian cities of Genoa, Livorno and Savona connect Corsica from the north and east, while ferry services from Nice, Toulon or Marseille serve the island from mainland France. Our route takes us north from Bastia. We first circle the northern peninsula of Cap Corse, mainly on beautiful coastal roads. Arriving in the west of the island, we cross the arid Désert des Agriates, an almost treeless area with a strong agricultural tradition. Navigating between the coast and the mountains of the island's interior, we advance in a wide arc to the area around the city of Calvi, where particularly wild, winding roads lead down to the Gulf of Porto, the end of our first stage.

337 KM • 6 STUNDEN // 210 MILES • 6 HOURS

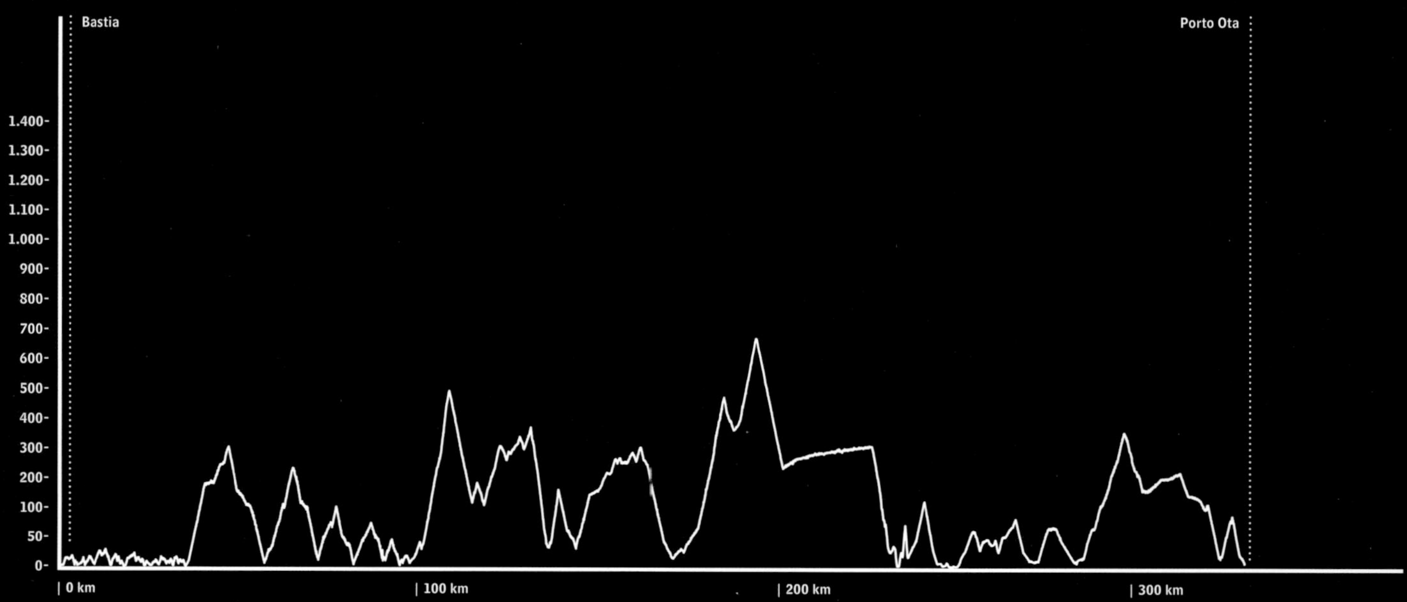

BASTIA
Calvi
AJACCIO
(AIACCIU)
Corte
(Corti)
C O R S E
Golfe de Porto
Golfe de Sagone
Golfe d'Ajaccio
Golfe de St-Florent
MER
TYRRHÉN
Parc Naturel
Régional
de la Corse
Désert des Agriates
Balagne
Filosorma
Niolo
Ville-di-Pietrabugno
(E Vile de Pietrabugnu)
San-Martino-di-Lota
Saint-Florent
Col de Vizzavona
Zicavo
(Zicavu)

PORTO OTA BONIFACIO

277 KM • 6 STUNDEN // 172 MILES • 6 HOURS

Sehnsucht. Süße, nagende Sehnsucht. Auf der langen Etappe rund ums Cap Corse, quer durch die Désert des Agriates und schließlich immer entlang der Westküste Korsikas haben wir uns gänzlich kurvensatt gefahren. Der innere Speicher ist voll mit Eindrücken aus diesem rauen, wunderschönen Land.

—

As we navigated the long stage around Cap Corse, across the Désert des Agriates and finally along the west coast of Corsica, we had our fill of curves, experiencing sweet, insistent longing for something different. Our memory is full of impressions from this rough, beautiful country.

PIANA D81

PIANA D81

Aber eines haben wir immer nur aus der Entfernung gesehen: das Meer. „Kaum zu glauben", ätzt der innere Strandurlauber in uns und rückt seinen Sonnenhut zurecht, „kaum zu glauben, dass du an allen Glücks-Oasen einfach vorübergefahren bist: den Buchten mit ihrem weißen Sand, den von Meeresrauschen und Chill-Out-Pop umhüllten Strandbars ..." – Kopfschüttelnd jagen wir den ewig cocktailschlürfenden Party-Bekannten früherer Teenage-Abenteuerjahre davon – und wissen dabei doch eines: Die Verlockungen des Beach-Lifestyle üben kaum noch Anziehungskraft aus, aber der mürbe Duft des Meeres verfolgt uns bereits in den Träumen. Einmal eintauchen und abtauchen, das muss sein. Freilich nicht im Badeenten-Modus an Touristen-Stränden, sondern im Vollkontakt. 360-Grad-3D-Meer, Vollwaschgang, Natur pur, das ist der Plan.

Im kleinen Porto Ota geht das auch nicht anders: Lediglich ein einsamer Streifen aus Sand und feinem Kies bietet sich für planschende Landratten an, wird von mächtigen Berghängen in einer engen Bucht in die Zange genommen. Badestrände sehen anders aus. Das Wasser eines kalten, grünen Gebirgsbachs hat hier einfach einen Pfropfen aus Sand abgeladen, nachdem er über lange Zeit hinweg das Tal am Meer mit Geröll gefüllt hat. Campervans suchen auf der Schotter-Fläche Schatten unter Bäumen, auf der anderen Seite des Taleinschnitts versammelt sich ein Grüppchen Häuser am Hang. Ein großer Fels versperrt den Blick auf die vorgelagerte Bucht und

But there was one thing we only ever saw from a distance: the sea. "Unbelievable," complains the inner beach-bum inside us, adjusting his sun hat. "I can't believe that you just drove past all these idyllic places: the bays with their white sand, the sound of the sea and chill-out pop at covered beach bars..." – Shaking our heads, we close our ears to the cocktail-sipping party animals of our teenage years. There's one thing we know for certain: the temptations of the beach lifestyle have little attraction anymore, although the tangy smell of the sea is already haunting us in our dreams. A plunge in the briny is definitely on the cards. Naturally we're not interested in the sanitized seaside experience available on tourist beaches. We're after full 360-degree contact. Nature at its purest, that's the plan.

In tiny Porto Ota we find exactly what we are looking for: a deserted strip of sand and fine gravel that is ideal for splashing landlubbers, pinched in by mighty mountain slopes in a narrow bay. The beaches look different here. The water from a cold, green mountain stream simply dumped a plug of sand here after filling the seaside valley with boulders. Campervans are seeking out shade under trees on the graveled area. A cluster of houses clings to a slope on the far side of the valley. A huge rock blocks the view of the bay in front of it and the solidly-built remnant of an old Genoese watchtower gazes out to sea. This is not an unusual setup in Corsica: the actual villages are located inland, while small seaside ports are

TO PLAGE D'ARONE

D757

oben spähen die bulligen Reste eines alten Genueser Wachturms aufs Meer hinaus. Auf Korsika ist das keine seltene Konstellation: Im Landesinneren liegen die eigentlichen Dörfer, am Meer verstecken sich kleine Häfen ewig misstrauisch vor Seeräubern und fremden Flotten. Die wechselnden Herrscher Korsikas haben selten im Gebirge Fuß gefasst, dafür aber mit Wachtürmen die Küsten gesichert.

Dabei ging es selten um den Schutz der einheimisch-korsischen Bevölkerung, sondern meist nur um den Schutz des besetzten Gebiets. Man kann in den viereckigen Wachturm auf dem Felsen oberhalb von Porto hineinsteigen, die Konstruktion ist typisch: Im Sockel gibt es keinen Zugang, erst auf halber Höhe öffnet sich eine kleine Tür. Früher mussten die Turmwächter mit einer Leiter hier hinaufklettern, konnten die bei herannahenden Feinden kurzerhand ins Innere ziehen und saßen dann sicher hinter den dicken Mauern. Heute gelangen Besucher auf einer modernen Stahltreppe zur alten Pforte und haben dann von der Turmkrone denselben Blick wie die Wächter des Mittelalters: über die Granitblöcke des Felsenbergs im Meer zum kleinen Hafen hinunter und ins üppig-grüne Tal des Landesinneren hinein. Nach Westen hat man die gesamte Bucht im Blick und schaut bis hinaus aufs offene Meer.

Dorthin soll es jetzt gehen: Unten im Hafen haben wir den Skipper eines Motorboots aufgetrieben, der uns zusammen mit ein paar Gleichgesinnten in die umgebende Felsenküste bringen wird. Mit entschlossenem Sprung geht es über die feisten Gummiwülste des Schlauchboots, kaum haben wir eine Halteschlaufe erwischt, knurrt im Heck des Bootes auch schon der Außenborder los. Vorsichtig schiebt das große Boot aus dem Hafen, tänzelt wenig später mit gurgelndem Motor übers Wasser der Bucht und beschleunigt schließlich hart. Fliegt, springt, röhrt dahin, scheint manchmal nur die Wellenkämme zu berühren, taucht dann wieder tief ins Wasser ein. Salzige Gischt wird in der Sonne zu vergänglichen Sekunden-Regenbögen, der Fahrtwind liegt wie ein feuchtes, warmes Tuch auf unserer Haut. Unter der Steilküste im Norden geht es hindurch, rund um Punta

always hidden away from suspicious pirates and foreign fleets. The ever-changing rulers of Corsica rarely gained a foothold in the mountains, but had to content themselves with securing the coast with watchtowers. This practice was seldom about safeguarding the native Corsican population, but usually only about protecting the occupied territory.

You can climb into the square watchtower on the rock above Porto. The construction methods are typical: there is no access at ground level, with just a small doorway halfway up. In the past, the tower guards had to climb up here by ladder, which they could quickly pull inside when the enemy approached, leaving them safely ensconced behind the thick walls. These days, visitors can climb a modern steel staircase to the old gate and then enjoy the same view from the top of the tower as the guardians of the Middle Ages: over the granite outcrops of the rocky mountain in the sea down to the small harbor and into the lush, green inland valley. To the west you have a view of the entire bay and can survey the open sea. That's where we're going next: down in the harbor we found the skipper of a motorboat who agrees to take us, along with a few like-minded people, to the surrounding rocky coast. With a determined jump, we cross over the thick rubber walls of the dinghy with barely enough time to catch a hand strap before the outboard motor starts growling in the stern of the boat.

The big boat gingerly pulls out of the harbor. A little later we find ourselves skipping across the water of the bay with the sound of the engine gurgling in our ears. Finally, the skipper accelerates hard and we're flying along, sometimes just seeming to touch the crests of the waves, then diving deep into the water again. The salty spray is transformed into fleeting rainbows in the sunlight and the wind lies on our skin like a warm, damp cloth. We pass beneath the cliffs in the north, around Punta Bianca and beyond the arch of the Arche de Purtellu, heading directly toward Monte Senino. The ocher pinnacles rear up out of the sea and at their base the boat glides more and more slowly into the shadow of a rock face. There it comes to rest on the waves, bucking, until the outboard engine falls silent.

HOTEL & RESTAURANT

HOTEL RESTAURANT DOLCE VITA
51 ROUTE DES ILES SANGUINAIRES
20000 AJACCIO
WWW.HOTEL-DOLCEVITA.COM

Bianca und vorbei am Felsbogen des Arche de Purtellu, direkt auf die ockergelben Zinnen des Monte Senino zu. Der türmt sich aus dem Meer auf, und an seinem Fuß gleitet das Boot immer langsamer werdend in den Schatten einer Felswand. Dort verharrt es unruhig auf den Wogen bockend, bis der Außenborder schweigt. Schließlich schwebt es nur noch in leichtem Drift auf der Wasseroberfläche, hebt und senkt sich im Rhythmus der Wellen, die gegen schrundige Klippen branden.

Mit ausgebreiteten Armen lassen wir uns nun im dunkelblauen Wasser treiben, lässige Flossenschläge schieben uns auf die Felsenküste zu. Sonnenstrahlen steigen von der Wasseroberfläche wie silbrige Scheinwerferbahnen hinab, werden aber tief unter uns vom Dunkel verschluckt. Die Wellen des Meeres schäumen an der Felswand, strudeln Myriaden von kleinen Luftbläschen ins Wasser. Fischschwärme taumeln selbstvergessen und anscheinend vollkommen schwindelfrei im ruhelos schwappenden Auf und Ab, Hin und Her der Brandung, schnappen hektisch nach staubgroßen Nahrungshäppchen. – Viel später, als wir glücklich lächelnd wieder vom Hafen hinaufgehen, schwingt die Unruhe des Meeres immer noch in uns. Salzkristalle kratzen auf der Haut, im Nacken hat sich ein leichter Sonnenbrand festgefressen und die Haare sind vom Meerwasser zu festen Strähnen verklebt. Der Duft von Jod liegt in der Luft, die Lippen schmecken salzig. „Endlich", denken wir, „endlich Meer".

Die D81 ist ein schmales Asphaltband, das zwischen Felswänden und einem kaum kniehohen Mäuerchen dahinwirbelt – auf der einen Seite das Gebirge, auf der anderen Seite der Sturz ins Meer. Wir fliegen unter Steineichen hindurch, wechseln unaufhörlich aus dem Schatten der Felswände in gleißendes Sonnenlicht und zurück. Dass der Asphalt die rötliche Farbe der umgebenden Felsen aufnimmt, und die Straße so noch mehr zu einem Element der Landschaft wird, fällt uns lange nicht auf. Wir sind einfach nur betört, hypnotisiert, inhaliert vom Flow dieser Straße, bewegen das Lenkrad mit versunkener Andacht. Unsere Fingerspitzen schlagen feine Synapsen ins Steuer, die dann in die Maschine hineinwachsen und durch deren Metall kriechen,

Eventually we float on the surface of the water in a slight drift, rising and falling to the rhythm of the surf crashing against the craggy cliffs.

We let ourselves drift in the dark blue water with outstretched arms. The occasional twist of our flippers pushes us towards the rocky coast. Sunbeams pierce the water's surface like silver headlights before being swallowed up by the darkness far below us. The foaming waves crash on the rock face, causing myriads of small air bubbles to whirl in the water. Shoals of fish tumble in the surf, snapping frantically for miniscule bits of food, oblivious and apparently completely free from giddiness in the restless back and forth movement. – Much later, as we walk back up from the port smiling happily, the restlessness of the sea still resonates with us. Salt crystals scratch the skin. We can feel slight sunburn on our necks and our hair is stuck together in stiff strands from the seawater. The scent of iodine pervades the air. Our lips taste salty. "Finally," we think, "finally we've made it to the sea."

The D81 is a narrow strip of asphalt that threads its way between rock faces and a little wall that is barely knee-high – on one side the mountains, on the other side a straight drop into the sea. We pass under holm oaks, constantly switching from the shadow of the cliffs to blazing sunlight and back again. We have long stopped noticing that the asphalt has taken on the reddish color of the surrounding rocks, making the road even more part of the landscape. We're simply infatuated, hypnotically enthralled by the flow of this road, turning the steering wheel with rapt devotion. Our fingertips unconsciously tap a finely calibrated signal to the steering wheel, which then feed into the machine, crawling through its metal until tentative feelers are placed on the road. Turn, feel the curve, counterturn. Inhale, exhale. A feeling of weightlessness sets in, even though we are subject to the laws of physics at all times, as gravity and kinetic energy perform a sensual dance cheek-to-cheek. At moments like this, the road itself becomes the medium and we find ourselves calling on ancient spirits to join our arcane story. They respond in kind: dusty rock giants stagger

HOTELS

CASANGHJULINA
FIUMU D'OSO
357 STRADA DI PURETTA
20137 PORTO-VECCHIO
WWW.CASANGHJULINA.COM

bis sie tastende Fühler auf die Fahrbahn legen. Einlenken, Kurve spüren, Auslenken. Ein- und Ausatmen. Schwerelosigkeit macht sich breit, obwohl wir die ganze Zeit im Koordinatensystem der Physik schwingen, Erdanziehungskraft und Bewegungsenergie im sinnlichen Engtanz.

Die Straße wird in solchen Momenten zum Medium, die Fahrt zur Kult-Handlung, wir rufen alte Geister. Und die kommen tatsächlich: Staubige Felsriesen wanken aus den Hängen, grüne Kräuterfeen und Quellnixen huschen durchs Zwielicht der Macchia, Ruinen-Reste, gemauerte Quellmündungen und terrassierte Felder raunen Geschichten aus grauer Vorzeit. Weit schwingt die Straße so in einem Tagtraum dahin, in großen Zügen über das Gebirge des Westens. Immer wieder kommt sie der Felsenküste ganz nahe, nur um dann wieder von ihr abzurücken, so weit, dass vom Meer in der Ferne nur eine dunstige Ahnung bliebt. Mal windet sich die D81 durch Täler und Wald, dann fliegt sie wieder in weiten Bögen hoch oben auf offenen Kuppen dahin.

In Ajaccio, der Hauptstadt Korsikas, packen wir uns eine bunte Eruption an Erinnerungen als Reisesouvenir ein: Boulespieler auf Plätzen unter Platanen, Palmen, die aus schattigen Hinterhöfen in einen azurblauen Himmel aufragen, enge Altstadtgassen mit Fassaden in Ocker, Orange und Beige, im Hafen ankernde Kreuzfahrtschiffe, Kapellen, Paläste und Kirchen. Wieder geht es dann in die Berge, hinunter in die Gegend um Pietrosella und dann zum ersten Mal hinein ins Landesinnere. Korsika hat unzählige Berggipfel, die über 2.000 Meter hoch sind, und in deren hochalpinen Raum dringen wir nun vor.

Bis Zicavu, dann geht es an der Westflanke des 1.745 Meter hohen Castellu d'Ornucciu nach Süden, bei Aullène schließlich auf die D420. Die haut nun ganz lässig die wunderbaren Bergpässe des Col de la Tana und Col de Saint-Eustache raus, und wird bei Bicchisano zum Zuträger der T40. Mit dieser Route haben wir für die heutige Etappe unsere letzte Begleiterin gefunden. Rollen über sie an der Bucht von Propriano zurück ans Meer, schneiden dann erneut im Landesinneren eine große Tranche der Westküste ab und landen schließlich bei Bonifacio an der Südspitze Korsikas.

Weit schwingt die Straße so in einem Tagtraum dahin, in großen Zügen über das Gebirge des Westens. Immer wieder kommt sie der Felsenküste ganz nahe, nur um dann wieder von ihr abzurücken, so weit, dass vom Meer in der Ferne nur eine dunstige Ahnung bliebt.

The road swings broadly, lost in a daydream, sweeping across the mountains to the west. Again and again it nears the rocky coast, only to switch away from it again, so that only a hazy inkling of the sea in the distance remains.

from the slopes, green woodland fairies and water sprites scurry through the twilight of the dense vegetation and the remains of ruins, walled spring mouths and terraced fields whisper stories from the distant past. The road swings broadly, lost in a daydream, sweeping across the mountains to the west. Again and again it nears the rocky coast, only to switch away from it again, so that only a hazy inkling of the sea in the distance remains. Sometimes the D81 winds through valleys and forest, then it rises up again in wide arcs onto open hilltops.

In Ajaccio, the capital of Corsica, we pack a colorful collection of memories as travel souvenirs: boules players in the squares under the shade of the plane trees, palm trees rising from secluded courtyards into an azure sky, narrow old town streets with facades painted in ochre, orange and beige, cruise ships at anchor in the port, chapels, palaces and churches. Once again we climb into the mountains, then down into the area around Pietrosella and finally inland for the first time. Corsica has countless mountain peaks that are over 2,000 meters high, and we are now entering the high alpine region.

We travel as far as Zicavu, then south on the west flank of the 1,745 meter high Castellu d'Ornucciu, finally joining the D420 at Aullène. This road casually encompasses the wonderful mountain passes of the Col de la Tana and Col de Saint-Eustache, and feeds into the T40 at Bicchisano. This is the last road on today's stage. We use it to get back to the sea at the Bay of Propriano, then cut off a large tranche of the west coast again by moving inland and finally end up at Bonifacio on the southern tip of Corsica.

HOTEL & RESTAURANT

SANTATERESA HOTEL
QUARTIER SAINT-FRANÇOIS
20169 BONIFACIO
WWW.HOTEL-SANTATERESA.COM

L'AUBERGE CORSE
MNT SAINT-ROCH
20169 BONIFACIO

DOMANIE DI MURTOLI
VALLÉE DE L'ORTOLO
20100 SARTÈNE
WWW.MURTOLI.COM

PORTO OTA BONIFACIO

Surf and Turf – das könnte als Motto der Etappe entlang der Westküste Korsikas taugen. Immer wieder zieht uns das Mittelmeer magisch an, wir entdecken die Schönheit unzähliger Buchten und Steilküsten. Die Streckenführung hält dabei meist einen topografisch bedingten Sicherheitsabstand ein, wilde Küstengebirge machen den direkten Zugang zum Meer unmöglich – und wunderschön. In bester Aussichtslage fahren wir vom Startpunkt am Golf von Porto auf steilen Klippen nach Süden und verschwinden dann immer wieder in den Bergen des Landesinneren. Erst rund um die Mündung des Flusses Liamone ist das Land flach, hinüber in die korsische Hauptstadt Ajaccio geht es dann aber wieder kurvig weiter. Mit einem Abstecher ins hochalpine Landesinnere setzen wir einen abenteuerlichen Akzent, über Propriano und Sartène geht es zurück an die Küste. Nach einem weiten Bogen um das Küstengebirge am „Punta Di Capuneru“ sowie den Meeresarm bei Figari landen wir in Bonifacio, hier haben wir die Südspitze Korsikas erreicht.

—

Surf and turf could be the motto of the stage that follows the west coast of Corsica. Again and again the Mediterranean attracts us magically, as we discover the beauty of countless bays and cliffs. Topographical features mean that the route usually keeps a safe distance, as wild coastal mountains make direct access to the sea impossible, but make up for this with their beauty. From our starting point on the Gulf of Porto, we head south on steep cliffs, enjoying the best panoramic position, and then disappear over and over again into the mountains of the interior of the country. The only flat part of the island is the area around the mouth of the Liamone River, which then becomes hilly again as we near the Corsican capital, Ajaccio. A detour into the high alpine interior of the country lends a touch of adventure to our journey as we return to the coast via Propriano and Sartène. After following a wide arc around the coastal mountains at “Punta Di Capuneru” and the estuary at Figari, we end up in Bonifacio at the southern tip of Corsica.

277 KM • 6 STUNDEN // 172 MILES • 6 HOURS

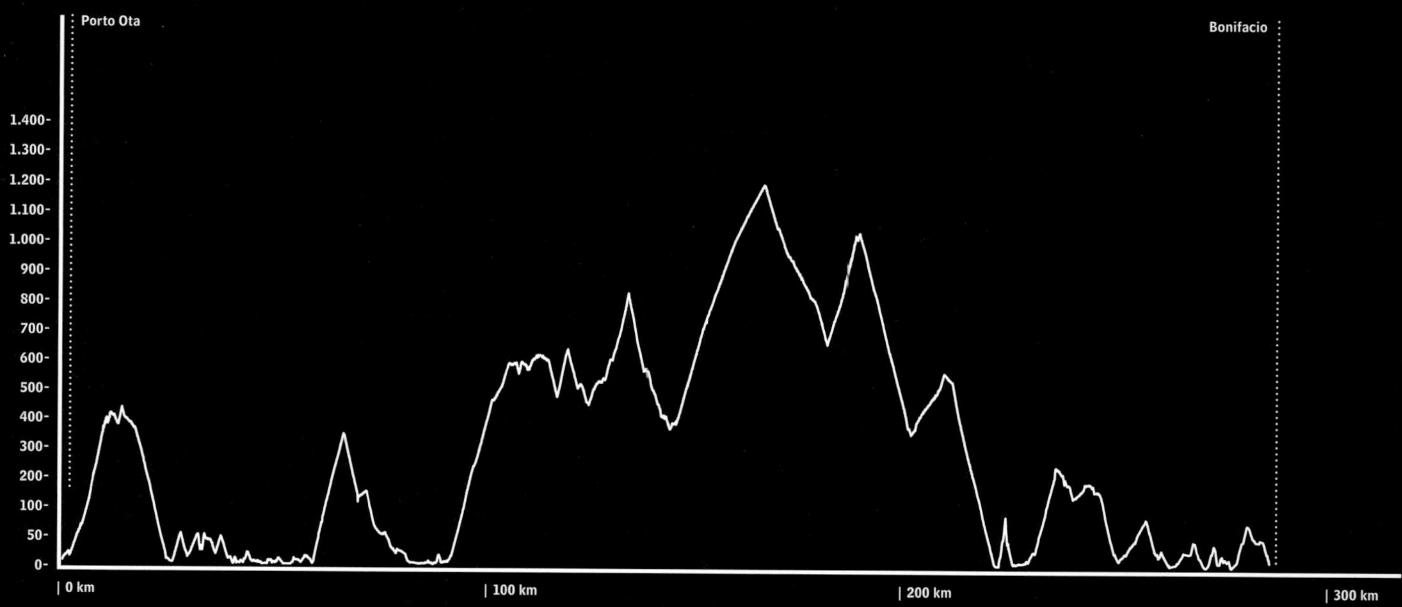

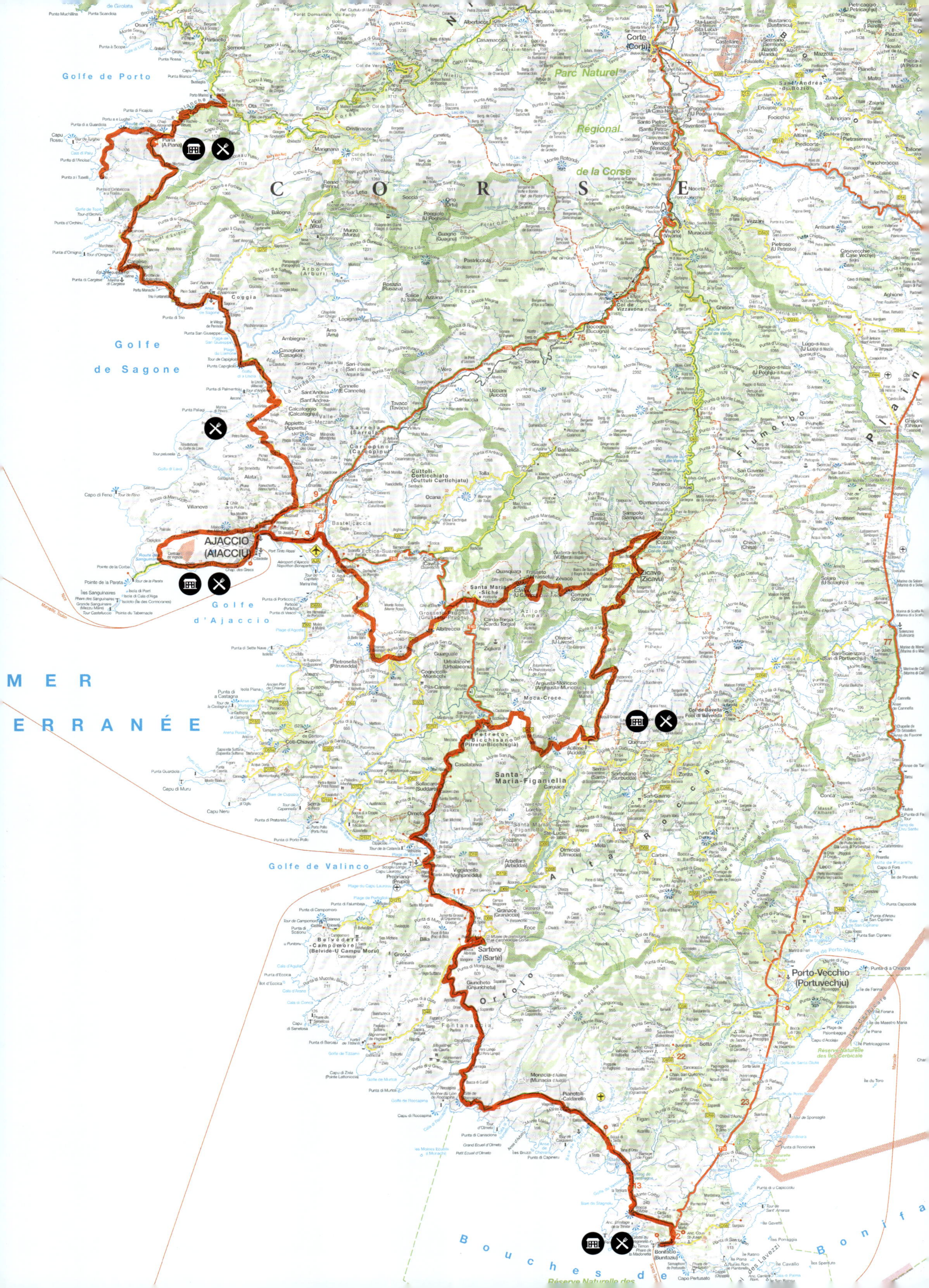
Golfe de Porto
Golfe de Sagone
Golfe d'Ajaccio
Golfe de Valinco
MER
ERRANÉE
C O R S E
Parc Naturel
Régional
de la Corse
Corte (Corti)
AJACCIO (AIACCIU)
Porto-Vecchio (Portuvecchju)
Sartène (Sartè)
Bonifacio (Bunifaziu)
Propriano (Prupià)
Piana (A Piana)
Cargèse
Zicavo (Zicavu)
Santa-Maria-Figaniella
Petreto-Bicchisano (Pitretu-Bicchisgià)
Bouches de Bonifacio
Réserve Naturelle des

T10

BONIFACIO
VIVARIO

288 KM • 5 STUNDEN // 179 MILES • 5 HOURS

Unten im Süden zerfasert Korsika im türkisgrünen Mittelmeer. Sandige Buchten haben sich zwischen Felsen eingenistet, weiche Kalkstöcke türmen sich auf einen harten Granitsockel. Kleine Inseln lagern sich an manchen Stellen vor die Küstenlinie, dazwischen liegen Sandbänke und Riffe unter der leuchtenden Wasseroberfläche.

—

Down south, Corsica's coastline frays in the turquoise-green Mediterranean Sea. Sandy bays have formed between the rocks, soft limestone stacks pile up on a hard granite base. Small islands lie just off the coast in some places, with sandbanks and reefs lying in between just beneath the luminous surface of the water.

D59

D59

LAC DE L'OSPEDALE

HOTEL & RESTAURANT

L'AUTHENTIQUE
RTE DE LEVIE
20124 ZONZA

HÔTEL RESTAURANT L'AIGLON
RUE PRINCIPALE
20124 ZONZA
WWW.HOTEL-ZONZA.COM

AUBERGE A PIGNATA
ROUTE DU PIANU
20170 LEVIE
WWW.APIGNATA.COM

Rund um die Südspitze Korsikas geht das so, von Bonifacio bis zur Île de Cavallo. Tagelang könnte man sich in dieser sonnenüberfluteten, windzerzausten Gegend herumtreiben und zusehen, wie einem Schwimmflossen zwischen Fingern und Fußzehen wachsen.

Aber wir haben ja etwas anderes vor: Die Berge der Südhälfte Korsikas sind heute unser Revier und das Ziel liegt oben in Vivario, am Fuß des nördlichen Hauptmassivs. Die Strecke ist also weit, aber wir haben unbändige Lust, endlich tief in die Berge zu fahren, die uns die ganze Zeit über in der Ferne verfolgt haben. Und die ersten Kilometer gehen leicht: Fast schnurgerade schneidet die T10 hinter Bonifacio nach Norden, nur wenige Male muss sie sich durch ein querlaufendes Flusstal winden oder die Hänge eines Weinbergs kreuzen. Bis nach Porto-Vecchio könnte das so weitergehen, aber ganz so leicht wollen wir es uns dann doch nicht machen. An der unscheinbaren Kreuzung der D59 biegen wir nach links ab und folgen dem zuerst vollkommen unspektakulär voranstrebenden Sträßchen. Bald schon sind wir in einem wildromantischen Hügelland unterwegs, in dem struppiges Buschwerk weitläufige Täler füllt, kleine Mäuerchen zugewucherte Gärten oder Schafweiden einfassen und sich massige Felsriegel neben der Straße herschieben. Hinter dem kleinen Chera geht es in ein paar weiten Schwüngen den Berg hinauf, dann landet die Straße bei Sotta in einem weitläufigen Tal.

Nun sind die nördlich aufsteigenden Hügel unser Ziel, bald liegt die Ebene hinter uns ein paar Stockwerke tiefer. Immer dichter packt sich das Gebirge mittlerweile um uns, bald geht der Straße der Platz aus und sie presst sich auf ihrer Bahn durch kleine Tunnelröhren, zirkelt dann auf Zehenspitzen im engen Tal bergauf, schraubt sich immer höher und landet schließlich an der Passhöhe des Col de Bacino. Fette Geröllkugeln liegen hier rechts und links der Straße im Gebüsch, die Straße lupft auf der Kuppe kurz den Gasfuß und schnürt dann ohne großes Federlesen auf der anderen Seite bergab. Im selben Rhythmus wie zuvor geht es weiter. Mal ist die Strecke kerzengerade in die Hügelflanken gefräst, durchtrennt

You'll find all this and more around the southern tip of Corsica, from Bonifacio to the Île de Cavallo. You could spend days lounging in this sun-drenched, windswept area, watching as you grow webbed fingers and toes.

But we have something quite different in mind: the mountains of the southern part of Corsica are our territory for today and our final destination is high up in Vivario, at the foot of the northern main massif. We have a long road ahead, but we are driven by an irrepressible desire to finally penetrate deep into the mountains that have been following us at a distance all this time. The first few kilometers are easy enough: the T10 carves a line almost dead straight north behind Bonifacio, only winding a few times when it encounters a transverse river valley or when crossing the slopes of a vineyard. We could continue on like this as far as Porto-Vecchio, but we don't want to make things too easy for ourselves. At the inconspicuous crossroads of the D59 we turn left and follow a little road that is quite unspectacular at first. Soon we are passing through wild and romantic hilly countryside, where scrubby bushes fill extensive valleys, little walls border overgrown gardens or sheep pastures and massive rocks push up along the roadside. Beyond the little village of Chera we swing up the mountain in a few wide curves, then the road ends up in a broad valley at Sotta. The hills rising to the north are our next goal and soon we find ourselves high above the plain.

The mountains begin to close in around us, forcing the road to squeeze its way through small tunnels, subsequently tiptoeing uphill in the narrow valley, spiraling higher and higher and finally emerging at the mountain pass of the Col de Bacino. Corpulent boulders sprawl in the bushes to the right and left of the road, which accelerates briefly over the mountain crest and then rushes down the other side without further ado. We continue in the same rhythm as before. Sometimes the route cuts straight into the hillsides, boring through layers of rock, the edges of which are now slowly eroding into dust in sunlight and heat, rain, snow and cold. Sometimes the route meanders and

D368

D268

Schichten von Gestein, dessen Schnittkanten nun in Sonnenlicht und Hitze, Regen, Schnee und Kälte langsam zu Staub erodieren. Mal schlängelt sie sich plätschernd dahin, schwingt und wedelt, schlingt sich um Hügelflanken, wirft sich ausgelassen ins Land. Und mal landet sie in den kleinen Weilern und Dörfern, die oft nur wenige Häuser groß sind: Carbini, Levie, San-Gavino-di-Carbini, Zonza.

Klingt alles überhaupt nicht französisch? – Dieser Eindruck täuscht nicht. Das Korsische ist aus Italien geprägt, die korsische Sprache – obwohl ganz eigen – mit dem Toskanischen verwandt. Und ja, das gilt auch fürs Essen. Irgendwann schlenzen wir das Auto auf den Parkplatz eines Dorf-Restaurants, lassen uns in die Stühle sinken und stöbern zunehmend verzückt in der Speisekarte. Dass sich in der korsischen Küche italienische und spanische Einflüsse vermischen, provenzalische Einflüsse und die Geschmäcker und Düfte arabischer Herkunft aufeinandertreffen, kann in den ländlichen Restaurants besonders gut erlebt werden. Über allem schwebt aber tatsächlich ein italienischer Esprit, eine bodenständige Leichtigkeit und Unkompliziertheit, die selbst deftigem „Comfort-Food" subtile Anmut verleiht.

„Eigentlich ist Korsika genau wie die korsische Küche", mampft irgendwann einer der Reisegefährten, „hier ist alles so herrlich handfest und ungekünstelt. Mit Charakter und gleichzeitig Schönheit gemacht." – Dem könnte der Rest der Reisegesellschaft von Herzen zustimmen – wenn sie nicht gerade mit Schlemmen beschäftigt wäre. Besonderheiten? Vielleicht, dass die Korsen eine spürbare Liebesbeziehung zu den Kräutern der Berge pflegen: Da schmeichelt der Rosmarin, liebkosen Lavendel und Myrte, pfeffert der Wacholder und schmust wilder Thymian. Je näher man dem Meer kommt, umso weiter nach oben rücken Meeresfrüchte und Fisch auf den Speisekarten – besonders hingerissene Gourmets sollen sogar schon von der korsischen „Aziminu", einer Fischsuppe, zu der geröstetes Brot mit einer deftigen Knoblauchsauce gereicht wird, in eine tiefe Abhängigkeit getrieben worden sein. Trotzdem spielt das Meer auf der Insel Korsika

snakes, swinging and twisting, wrapping itself around hillsides, throwing itself exuberantly into the embrace of the surrounding countryside. And sometimes it takes us into tiny hamlets and villages, which often consist of just a few houses: Carbini, Levie, San-Gavino-di-Carbini, Zonza.

You might thing this doesn't sound very French at all. – And you'd be quite right. Culturally Corsica is closer to Italy. The Corsican language – although quite unique – is related to Tuscan. The same goes for the food too. At some point we pull into the parking lot of a village restaurant, sink into our chairs and browse the menu with increasing ecstasy. The fact that Italian and Spanish influences mix in Corsican cuisine, that Provençal influences and the flavors and aromas of Arabia meet, is particularly evident in the rural restaurants. However, the spirit of Italy really does hover over everything, a down-to-earth lightness and simplicity that lends even hearty "comfort food" a subtle grace.

"Actually, Corsica is just like Corsican cuisine," one of our traveling companions manages to say at some point, through his mouthful of food. "Everything is so wonderfully down-to-earth and natural here. It's all made with character and beauty." – The rest of the group would wholeheartedly agree – if they weren't so busy eating. Particular characteristics? Perhaps that the Corsicans are clearly in love with the herbs of the mountains: the caress of rosemary caresses, the tender brush of lavender and myrtle, the tang of juniper and the embrace of wild thyme. The closer you get to the sea, the higher seafood and fish move up the menu – some particularly enthusiastic gourmets are said to have become addicted to Corsican "Aziminu", a fish soup that is served with toasted bread with a hearty garlic sauce.

Nevertheless, from a purely culinary point of view, on the island of Corsica the sea plays second fiddle to pork, the true star of the kitchen. Semi-wild pigs are allowed to fatten themselves mainly on a diet of sweet chestnuts. This not only makes them incredibly tasty, but also quite lean as the fitness regime imposed by the terrain means

HOTEL & RESTAURANT

PARAD'ISULA SANTA GIULIA
PARADISULA PLAGE DE
20137 PORTO-VECCHIO

HÔTEL U CAPU BIANCU
DOMAINE DE POZZONIELLO
20169 BONIFACIO
WWW.UCAPUBIANCU.COM

LE PETIT CHOSE PALOMBAGGIA
FOLACCA, RTE DE PALOMBAGGIA
20137 PORTO-VECCHIO

D69

rein kulinarisch betrachtet die zweite Geige, der wahre Küchenstar ist das Schwein. Halbwilde Rüsseltiere mästen sich hier angeblich absichtlich und vorwiegend von Edelkastanien, werden so unglaublich schmackhaft, legen sich aber durch Fitness-Übungen im harten Gelände eine lediglich ganz magere Fettschicht auf die Rippen. Schließlich stürzen sie sich dann mit Hingabe zum Beispiel in die „Canneloni au Brocciu", eine mit Gemüse und Schweinefleisch gefüllte Nudelrolle – zumindest servieren uns das korsische Patrioten in weinseliger Stimmung als Erklärung für die unfassbare Köstlichkeit korsischer Schweinefleischgerichte.

Wie die Wildschweine in die Salami kommen, wird dann nicht erklärt, man lenkt uns an dieser Stelle gezielt mit anderen Gaumenfreuden vom gründlicherer Recherche ab. Ein „Stufatu" landet auf dem Tisch, lässt Lammfleisch, Zwiebeln, Nudeln und Käse dampfen, danach versagen aus Ziegen- und Schafsmilch hergestellte Käsesorten gründlich dabei, uns final den Magen zu schließen. Schwer angeschlagen und gleichermaßen glückselig verlassen wir irgendwann das Restaurant, um uns an die entscheidenden

they put on only a very meager layer of fat on their ribs. The meat is served in "Canneloni au Brocciu", tubes of pasta filled with vegetables and pork – at least that's what some wine-loving Corsican patriots tell us in explanation of the incredible delicacy of Corsican pork dishes. We never get to hear how the wild boar gets into the salami because at this point we are deliberately distracted from more thorough research with other delicacies. A "Stufatu" lands on the table, steaming lamb, onions, pasta and cheese, after which cheeses made from goat and sheep's milk finally fill us to bursting. Vanquished but happy, we leave the restaurant at some point to start the crucial final kilometers of our journey, the last leg down to the sea at Porto-Vecchio. For a bowl of Aziminu, of course...

The mushroom-shaped bay of Saint Cyprien – or San Cipri-anu in Corsican – with its long sandy beach is very tempting, but we stay the course. We turn off at Sainte-Lucie for Conca, land at Favone one last time on the coast and finally make our way back inland in Solenzara. We end up, completely dizzy, at the starting point of the coastal loop in Zonza. It may be an unfortunate fact that the restaurants

Kilometer der Fahrt zu machen, den Schlenker hinunter ans Meer nach Porto-Vecchio. Aziminu, Sie wissen schon ... Die pilzförmige Bucht von Saint Cyprien – oder korsisch: San Ciprianu – mit ihrem langen Sandstrand lockt wirklich sehr, aber wir bleiben auf Kurs. Biegen bei Sainte-Lucie in Richtung Conca ab, landen bei Favone ein letztes Mal erneut an der Küste und machen uns erst in Solenzara endgültig auf den Weg zurück ins Landesinnere. Am Ende landen wir völlig schwindlig gefahren am Ausgangspunkt des Küstenloops in Zonza. Dass nun gerade die Mittagspause der Restaurants beginnt, mag eine betrübliche Tatsache sein, trägt aber auch dazu bei, einen anderen Appetit anzufachen – den auf Kurven.

Bis Aullène stürmen wir, dann sind wir auf bekanntem Terrain: Hier sind wir auf der vorherigen Etappe bereits gewesen und fahren die D59 nun in umgekehrter Richtung, von Süd nach Nord, von Aullène über den Col de la Vaccia bis nach Zicavo. Erst hier ist die Streckenführung neu für uns, die D69 führt uns weiter nach Norden ins Gebirge. Zuerst verändert sich wenig, bis Cozzano und darüber hinaus breitet sich die raue Macchie der Berge aus, aber dann schleicht sich langsam eine Ahnung von Hochgebirge ins Bild. Die Vegetation wird dünner und härter, Nadelbäume ersetzen das Strauchwerk, die Eichen und Kastanien des weiter unten liegenden Lands.

Auch an der Straße haben die Kälte und das raue Wetter der Höhenlage gefressen, immer öfter wirken die Ränder löchrig. Ab der Grenze zum Departement Haute-Corse ist die Ansage dann deutlich: Willkommen im Hochgebirge. Über Ghisoni fliegen wir weiter, schrauben uns dann in den Serpentinen am Col de Sorba empor, dann strandet die D69 atemlos und vom Fahrtwind zerzaust an der großen Kreuzung mit der T20 bei Vivario. Ende der Etappe. Und wie es der Zufall will, öffnen gerade wieder die Restaurants. Glück muss man haben.

Am Ende landen wir völlig schwindlig gefahren am Ausgangspunkt des Küstenloops in Zonza. Dass nun gerade die Mittagspause der Restaurants beginnt, mag eine betrübliche Tatsache sein, trägt aber auch dazu bei, einen anderen Appetit anzufachen – den auf Kurven.

We end up, completely dizzy, at the starting point of the coastal loop in Zonza. It may be an unfortunate fact that the restaurants are about to serve lunch, but this also helps to whet our appetite for curves.

are about to serve lunch, but this also helps to whet our appetite for curves.

We storm up as far as Aullène, then we're on familiar territory: we've already been here on a previous stage and are now taking the D59 in the opposite direction, from south to north, from Aullène via the Col de la Vaccia to Zicavo. The route only becomes new to us at this point. The D69 takes us further north into the mountains. At first little changes until we reach Cozzan. The rough maquis of the mountains spreads out beyond, but then slowly high mountains creep into the picture. The vegetation thins and coarsens, with conifers replacing the shrubs, oaks and sweet chestnuts of the countryside below.

The cold and the rough weather at this high altitude have eaten away at the road, too, and the edges are becoming more and more scrappy. As we cross the border into the Departement of Haute-Corse, the message is clear: welcome to the highlands. We fly through Ghisoni, then wind our way up the serpentine bends at the Col de Sorba, at which point the D69 comes to a breathless halt, tossed by the wind at the major intersection with the T20 at Vivario, where this stage of our trip comes to an end. As luck would have it, the restaurants are opening again. Fortune favors the bold.

HOTEL & RESTAURANT

HOTEL - RESTAURANT & SPA
E CASELLE
LIEU-DIT AGNIUDIPINO
20231 VENACO
WWW.HOTELECASELLE.COM

BONIFACIO VIVARIO

Die Ostküste Korsikas ist deutlich ruhiger und weniger zerklüftet als der Westen, das Land ist flacher und die Strände breit. Was für Badeurlauber großen Reiz haben mag, ist auf der Suche nach Kurvenstraßen natürlich kein ideales Terrain. Auf unserer dritten Etappe verlassen wir die Küste daher zum ersten Mal für lange Zeit und fahren durchs Landesinnere des Südens der Insel. Beim kleinen Städtchen Zonza angekommen, legen wir aber trotzdem eine Schleife in Richtung des Meeres ein, verbinden die Fahrt über spektakuläre Bergstraßen mit einer kurzen Stippvisite an der Ostküste: Bei Porto-Vecchio sowie zwischen Favone und Solenzara weiter nördlich schnuppern wir ein letztes Mal Seeluft. Danach geht es im Solenzara-Tal und durch die nachgelagerten Canyons zurück nach Zonza, von hier aus weiter nach Aullène. Hier treffen wir auf ein Teilstück der Route unserer letzten Etappe, ab Zicavo sind wir aber wieder auf Neuland unterwegs. Über Cozzano geht es zur Grenze des Departements Haute-Corse und dann weiter ins Hochgebirge Korsikas. Am Etappenziel in Vivario haben wir die höchsten Berge Korsikas in Reichweite, so liegt beispielsweise der 2.389 Meter hohe Monte d'Oro auf dem Gebiet von Vivario.

—

The east coast of Corsica is much quieter and less rugged than the west, the land is flatter and the beaches are broad. Although this may be appealing to beach holidaymakers, it is, of course, not ideal terrain when you're looking for winding roads. On our third stage we therefore leave the coast for a long period for the first time and drive through the interior of the south of the island. Arriving at the small town of Zonza, we still make a loop in the direction of the sea, combining the drive over spectacular mountain roads with a short flying visit to the east coast: near Porto-Vecchio and between Favone and Solenzara further north we breathe in the salt sea air one last time. We then carry on to the Solenzara valley and through the canyons beyond back to Zonza and from there on to Aullène. Here we rejoin a section of the route from our previous stage, but once we reach Zicavo we are on terra nova once again. Passing though Cozzano we reach the border of the Departement of Haute-Corse and then move further into the high mountains of Corsica. The highest mountains in Corsica are within reach at our destination in Vivario, for example the 2,389 meter high Monte d'Oro is close by.

288 KM • 5 STUNDEN // 179 MILES • 5 HOURS

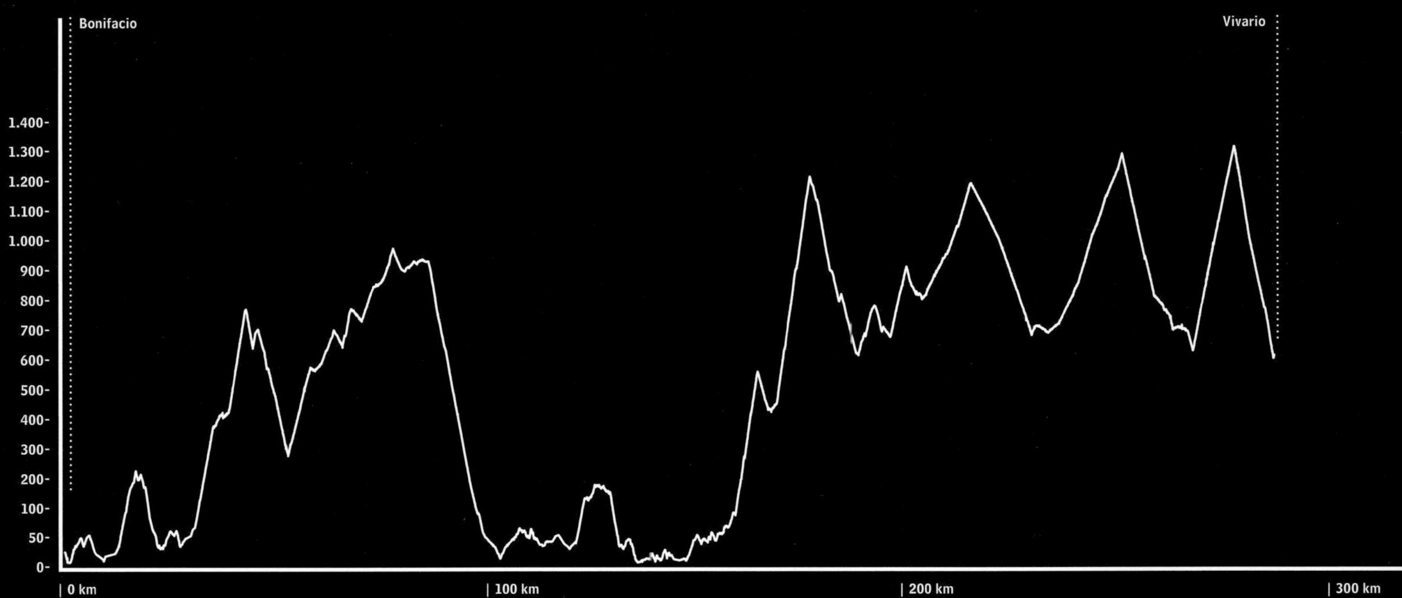

MER
TYRRHÉNI
Bouches de
Bonifacio
Golfe de Valinco
Porto-Vecchio
(Portuvechju)
Sartène
(Sartè)
Zicavo
(Zicavu)
Quenza
Santa-Maria-Figaniella
Alta Rocca
Ortolo
Fiumorbo
Plaine Orientale
Petreto-Bicchisano
(Pitretu-Bicchisgià)
Cuttoli-Corticchiato
(Cuttuli Curtichjatu)
Vizzavona
Régional
de la Corse
Bonifacio
(Bunifaziu)

VIVARIO
CORTE

197 KM • 4 STUNDEN // 123 MILES • 4 HOURS

Aufwachen in Vivario, im Obergeschoss Korsikas. Ringsum lässt eine sommerliche Mittelmeersonne die Berggipfel schwitzen, während sich in die Schatten zwischen den Steinhäusern noch eine gebirgige Nachtkühle schmiegt. Platanenblattdächer flimmern in einer sanften Brise, üppige Hortensien fluten über Terrassenmauern und Oleander vertritt selbst im wechselhaften Klima des Gebirges standhaft den Süden.

—

We wake up on the top floor of our accommodation in Vivario, Corsica. All around us the Mediterranean summer sun blasts the mountain peaks, while the remains of the cool night air hover in the shadows between the stone houses. Sycamore leaf canopies shimmer in a gentle breeze, lush hydrangeas spill over terrace walls, and the oleanders face steadfastly southwards even in the varying climate of the mountains.

Fensterläden in weiß und braun und grün werden an wettergegerbten Häusern zu klimpernden Augenlidern, rostige Balkongitterstäbe klammern sich an Fassaden, deren gelegentliches Bröckeln von Weinranken lyrisch begleitet wird. Bis zum Horizont breiten sich in der Umgebung Granitriesen aus, die ihre Körper mit dichtem, grünem Pelz bedecken und kahle, graue Häupter in einen blauen Himmel strecken.

So sieht ein guter Morgen aus, denkst du, während etwas in dir mit den in lasziver Zeitlupe dahinflauschenden Wolken auf Reise geht. Tiefenentspannt und stetig. Aus dem Café im Erdgeschoss steigen herrliche Düfte, und genau dahin wirst du jetzt hinuntersteigen. Irgendwann später soll es natürlich weitergehen, auf die Reise über die Berge, aber das hat Zeit. Jetzt schlagen wir erst einmal Wurzeln in den Fels des korsischen Gebirges, lassen die Zeit verstreichen, kosten sie so wirklich aus. – Dabei sind wir ja eigentlich auf rasantem Boden unterwegs, mit dieser Etappe ganz besonders. Immer wieder werden die Bergstraßen hier oben in Zehntelsekunden ausgelotet, als Höhepunkt der Rallye Korsika, die zu den besonders haarsträubenden Momenten des Rennsports gehört. Eigentlich ist ganz Korsika das Reich der Rallye, schließlich wurden und werden rund um die Insel Sonderprüfungen und Verbindungsetappen hingebrannt, mittlerweile macht auch eine Klassik-Rallye das Beste aus den korsischen Traumstraßen. Aber die Berge des Landesinneren sind eben die eigentlichen Hauptdarsteller: wilde und schmale Routen, die beinahe unlösbare Gleichungen ins Gelände kritzeln.

Heute haben wir uns vorgenommen, in diese Welt hineinzufahren und jeden Kilometer aus einer Perspektive mit Überrollkäfig, Semislicks, Stoppuhr unter die Lupe zu nehmen. Natürlich wird nur ein innerer Sekundenzeiger rasen, ohne offiziellen Rennsportauftrag lässt man das Fahren auf letzter und auch vorletzter Rille hier oben besser sein. Und das nicht nur, weil sich die korsische Gendarmerie auf bestimmten Streckenabschnitten besonders intensiv der Rennleitung und Zeitmessung widmet oder Gegenverkehr immer dann auftaucht, wenn einem sowieso gerade auch die Straße

Window shutters in white and brown and green become fluttering eyelids on weather-beaten houses, rusty balcony rails cling to romantically crumbling facades covered with vine tendrils. Granite giants spread out as far as the horizon here, covering their bulky bodies with thick, green fur and their bare, gray heads stretching into an azure sky.

This is what a good morning looks like, you think, while something inside you joins the fluffy clouds as they pass by in languorous slow motion, deeply relaxed and grounded. Wonderful aromas rise from the café on the ground floor, and that is exactly where we are headed right now. At some point, later in the day of course, we should continue, on the journey over the mountains, but that can wait. For the time being let's put down some roots in the rock of the Corsican mountains, taking our time to savor our surroundings. – This particlar stage of our trip is going to be all about speed. These mountain roads are a regular highlight of the Corsica Rally, one of the most hair-raising moments in high-speed motor racing. In fact, the whole of Corsica is a rally driver's dream, with special stages and connecting routes around the island. Meanwhile a classic rally also makes the best of the Corsica's dream roads. However, the mountains of the interior are the real protagonists: wild and narrow routes that carve almost impossibly puzzling equations into the terrain.

Today's plan is to explore this world and to test every kilometer as if our car was fitted with a roll cage and semi-slick tires and we were racing against the clock. Of course, this is all in the mind... The truth is that a definite level of self-control is vital here, not just because the Corsican police are particularly hot on catching speeding drivers on certain sections of the route, or because oncoming traffic always looms into view when you're running out of road anyway, but in particular for reasons of self-interest: Corsican mountain roads are no place for novices, leaving no room for carelessness or cockiness. If you are used to other routes that make certain allowances for mistakes, promoting flow and showing tolerance thanks to the skill of the road

ausgeht, sondern in besonderem Eigeninteresse: Korsische Gebirgsstraßen sind immer wieder nichts für Anfänger, nichts für Nachlässigkeit und schon gar nichts für Übermut. Wer von anderswo Streckenführungen gewohnt ist, die durch das Geschick der Straßenplaner und eine gewisse Offenheit des Terrains Platz für Fehler lassen, den Flow fördern und Toleranz zeigen, wird von Korsika überrascht sein. Hier bücken sich Straßen oft noch dem Diktat der Topografie. Streckenführung gibt es dann nur als unverfälschtes Extrakt der gewundenen Täler und schroffen Berge. Love it or leave it.

Da fährst du hellwach oder als Passagier der Straße, du fährst maßvoll oder im Zustand ständiger Überforderung. Nicht umsonst wurde das Ende der infamen Gruppe-B-Rallyemonster in den 1980er-Jahren auf Korsika eingeläutet. Selbst die haarscharf fahrenden Helden der Rallye-WM, deren Meisterschaft darin besteht kontrolliert zu eskalieren, waren von Korsika überfordert. Die entsetzlich schnellen Audi Sport Quattro S1, Ford RS200, MG Metro 6R4 oder Peugeot 205 Turbo 16 mit ihren bis zu 500 PS starken Motoren und bestialisch grippenden Allradantrieben fuhren so weit in entlegene Gegenden der Physik hinaus, dass nur minimale Fahrfehler fatale Folgen hatten: 1985 kostete die Korsika-Rallye Attilio Bettega im Lancia Rally 037 das Leben. Ein Jahr später riss ein Unfall auf der Portugal-Rallye drei Zuschauer in den Tod und verletzte weitere 31 Personen schwer, danach verunglückte der Finne Henri Toivonen samt seinem Beifahrer Sergio Cresto im Lancia Delta S4 zwischen Castirla und Corte. Wieder Korsika ... – Die Gruppe B schleppte sich danach mit heillosem Schrecken in den Knochen noch ans Ende der Rennsaison 1986, danach war für diese überzüchteten Auto-Megalomanen Schluss.

Mit diesem Wissen im Hinterkopf gehen wir die ersten Kilometer auf der T20 in Richtung Bocognano ganz kontrolliert an und werden vom hier noch ausgesprochen friedlichen Verlauf der Straße behutsam vorgewärmt. Elegant surft das Asphaltband dahin, ist recht breit und gut ausgebaut – das Tempo steigt ebenso unmerklich wie unaufhörlich. Irgendwann

planners and the openness of the terrain, a surprise lies in store for you on Corsica. Here, many roads still bend to the dictates of the topography. The route follows the winding valleys and rugged mountains. Love it or leave it. You need your wits about you on this road, driving moderately or in a constant state of strain. It was with good reason that that the infamous Group B rally monsters were flagged to a halt in Corsica in the 1980s. Despite the hair's-breadth precision of their driving and their sovereign control behind the wheel, even the heroes of the World Rally Championship were overwhelmed by Corsica.

The freakily fast Audi Sport Quattro S1, Ford RS200, MG Metro 6R4 or Peugeot 205 Turbo 16 with their up to 500 hp engines and ferocious all-wheel drives pushed the laws of physics so far that even the tiniest driving errors had fatal consequences: in 1985 the Corsica Rally cost Attilio Bettega his life in the Lancia Rally 037. A year later, an accident at the Portugal Rally killed three spectators and seriously injured another 31 people, after which the Finn Henri Toivonen and his co-driver Sergio Cresto crashed in the Lancia Delta S4 between Castirla and Corte. Corsica again... – Group B then limped on to the end of the 1986 racing season with a sense of terror in its bones, after which it was all over for these hyperpowered vehicles. With this in mind, we approach the first few kilometers on the T20 heading in the direction of Bocognano in a highly controlled manner and find ourselves in the warm embrace of the gentle course of the road. The broad and well-developed ribbon of asphalt curls along elegantly – our speed increases imperceptibly and incessantly.

At some point we explode in long arcs, racing along to the singing of our tires, letting the car do its work with relish before finally realizing that the Corsican cornering devil at our shoulder is laughing hard up his sleeve. All this craziness comes to an end at the junction with the D4 in the direction of Vero. We drive with restraint and with our eyes peeled. Finally, after just a few meters, the road starts to climb resolutely up the mountain, twisting into hairpin

zünden wir hart in langgezogene Bögen, reiben mit singenden Reifen dahin, lassen das Auto lustvoll arbeiten und merken erst spät, dass sich der korsische Kurventeufel auf unserer Schulter gerade heftig ins Fäustchen lacht. Am Abzweig der D4 in Richtung Vero ist damit definitiv Schluss, jetzt wird wieder mit Zurückhaltung und betont auf Sicht gefahren. Schließlich wirft sich die Straße bereits nach wenigen Metern entschlossen den Berg hinauf, knotet sich zu Kehren und Serpentinen, wird hinter Vero sogar noch wilder. Hier haben wir es, das atemberaubende Vorwärtsflackern korsischer Bergstraßen: Immer wieder perfekter Slalom, dann dreschen einem scharfe Tempowechsel im Flow der Straße Knüppel zwischen die Beine, es folgt hastiges Entknoten und Neusortieren.

Die Straße kurvt inzwischen in weit entfernte Bergtäler hinein, dicke Packungen von Piniennadeln bilden an den Straßenrändern im Schatten des Bergwalds immer wieder rutschige Auslaufzonen. Zwischen Azzana und Rezza knickt die D4 nach Westen ab, wedelt energiegeladen weiter bis Vico und gibt dort auf der Passhöhe des Col Saint Antoine den Staffelstab an die in Richtung Norden führende D70 ab. Mit ihr kehrt fürs Erste Ruhe ein: Immer wieder in herrlicher Aussichtslage segelt die Straße in sanftem Takt durchs Gebirge, schneidet über Renno bis zum Col de Sévi, rollt an Cristinacce vorbei, wechselt dann auf die D84 und landet nach wenigen Kilometern Fahrt am Fuß mächtiger Granitsockel. In einem bewaldeten Tal geht es nun zum Col de Vergio und weiter nach Albertacce, die massigen Felstürme zur Linken begleiten uns. Rechts ruht der Calacuccia-Stausee in seinem kiesigen Bett, nach Norden steigt das Gelände zum Massiv des 2.706 Meter hohen Monte Cinto auf, dem höchsten Berg Korsikas.

Und dann wird es grandios: Die D84 fräst sich durch den tief eingeschnittenen Canyon de la Ruda hinüber nach Castirla und

bends and serpentines, becoming ever wilder beyond Vero. This is it, the breathtaking roller-coaster ride of Corsica's mountain roads: perfect slalom patterns are repeated over and over again, before a sharp change in speed is dictated by the flow of the road, followed by hasty uncoiling and readjustment.

The road now curves into distant mountain valleys. Again and again, thickly packed mats of pine needles form slippery run-off zones on the roadside in the shade of the mountain forest. Between Azzana and Rezza, the D4 veers westwards, pushing energetically on to Vico and there, at the top of the Col Saint Antoine, hands over the baton to the northbound D70. Suddenly, peace reigns once again, for the time being at least: the panoramic road sails gently through the mountains, cutting through Renno to the Col de Sévi, rolling past Cristinacce, then switching to the D84 and, after a few kilometers, ends up at the foot of a powerful mass of granite. Passing through a wooded valley we proceed to the Col de Vergio and on to Albertacce, massively towering rock formations accompanying us on the left. To the right are the gravel shores of the Calacuccia reservoir, while to the north the terrain rises to the massif of the 2,706-meter high Monte Cinto, the highest mountain in Corsica.

Things suddenly take on an even more grandiose character: the D84 cuts its way through the deeply fissured Canyon de la Ruda as far as Castirla, where we change to the D18, heading south. There is nothing to indicate that Henri Toivonen crashed here, although there is no denying that this is the spot: surrounded by rock faces and little walls, the road shoots away from the abyss. If you were to hit the wall at excessive speed when exiting from a long left-hand bend, you'd never have time to adjust to the following hard right. Inevitably you would find yourself in an incredibly deep freefall, ending in a fireball.

D84

CANYON DE LA RUDA

Dass hier die Stelle des Crashs von Henri Toivonen liegt, ist nicht sofort zu erkennen – was passiert sein muss, dafür auf jeden Fall: Wie ein Kanal ballert die Straße umsäumt von Felswand und Mäuerchen vor dem Abgrund dahin. Wer hier mit Speed-Überschuss am Ausgang einer langgezogenen Linkskurve die Wand touchiert, bekommt das Ganze für die folgende, harte Rechts nicht mehr sortiert. Und hier geht es in freiem Flug unfassbar tief hinunter. Feuerball vorprogrammiert.

dort wechseln wir auf die D18 nach Süden. Dass hier die Stelle des Crashs von Henri Toivonen liegt, ist nicht sofort zu erkennen – was passiert sein muss, dafür auf jeden Fall: Wie ein Kanal ballert die Straße umsäumt von Felswand und Mäuerchen vor dem Abgrund dahin. Wer hier mit Speed-Überschuss am Ausgang einer langgezogenen Linkskurve die Wand touchiert, bekommt das Ganze für die folgende, harte Rechts nicht mehr sortiert. Und hier geht es in freiem Flug unfassbar tief hinunter. Feuerball vorprogrammiert.

Mit dieser Erinnerung machen wir uns auf die letzten Kilometer: runter nach Corte und dann zum Ausrollen die 16 Kilometer bis ans Ende des Tals von Restonica. Kühle, klare Bergluft schnuppern. Die Füße in glasig-grünen Bergbächen baden, die zwischen fetten Geröllbrocken ins Tal plätschern. Zusehen, wie eine warme Abendsonne in den hageren Kronen von Kiefern flirrt und romantische Scherenschnitte aus Licht und Schatten zaubert. Irgendwer fühlt sich an die Rocky Mountains erinnert, an die Wüstenberge Kaliforniens. Aber dass wir auf Korsika sind, kann man trotzdem bestimmt nicht vergessen.

There is nothing to indicate that Henri Toivonen crashed here, although there is no denying that this is the spot: surrounded by rock faces and little walls, the road shoots away from the abyss. If you were to hit the wall at excessive speed when exiting from a long left-hand bend, you'd never have time to adjust to the following hard right. Inevitably you would find yourself in an incredibly deep freefall, ending in a fireball.

With this in mind we start the last few kilometers down to Corte, then coasting the 16 kilometers to the end of the Restonica valley. We breathe in the cool, clear mountain air, stopping to bathe our feet in crystalline green mountain streams that trickle down into the valley between hulking boulders. We watch as the warm evening sun shimmers in the sparse crowns of pine trees and conjures up romantic silhouettes of light and shadow. Someone is reminded of the Rocky Mountains, the desert mountains of California. But you certainly can't forget that we're in Corsica.

VIVARIO CORTE

In der Nordhälfte der Insel finden sich die höchsten Berge Korsikas. Hier sind wir auf der vierten Etappe unterwegs, fahren rund um den „Parc naturel régional de Corse" und bis hinauf an den Fuß des Monte Cinto-Massivs. Im kleinen Weiler Vivario mit seinen knapp 500 Einwohnern geht es los, in weitem Bogen südlich des knapp 2.390 Meter hohen Monte d'Oro vorbei. Auf halbem Weg in die Küstenstadt Ajaccio biegen wir dann nach Norden ab, bis nach Vico in der Region Cruzzini. Auf dem weiteren Weg südlich des Monte Cinto überqueren wir immer wieder kleine Straßenpässe, stoßen auf einer Art Kreisbewegung bis nach Castirla, einer kaum 200 Einwohner großen Gemeinde am Fluss Golo, zwischen dem Monte Pinerole (1.951 m) und Monte Agatu (1.641 m). Ziel der Fahrt ist Corte, ein Abstecher ins wunderschöne Restonica-Tal rundet die Route auf den Spuren der Korsika-Rallye ab.

—

The highest mountains in Corsica are located in the northern half of the island. Here we are on the fourth stage, driving around the "Parc naturel régional de Corse" and as far as the foot of the Monte Cinto massif. We start out from the small hamlet of Vivario, population almost 500, following a wide arc south of Monte d'Oro, almost 2,390 meters high. Halfway to the coastal town of Ajaccio we then head north all the way to Vico in the Cruzzini region. Continuing south of Monte Cinto, we repeatedly cross small mountain pass roads, taking a kind of circuitous route to Castirla, a community with barely 200 inhabitants on the river Golo, between Monte Pinerole (1,951 m) and Monte Agatu (1,641 m). The final destination of our trip is Corte, while a detour to the beautiful Restonica valley rounds off the route, following the route of the Corsica Rally.

197 KM • 4 STUNDEN // 123 MILES • 4 HOURS

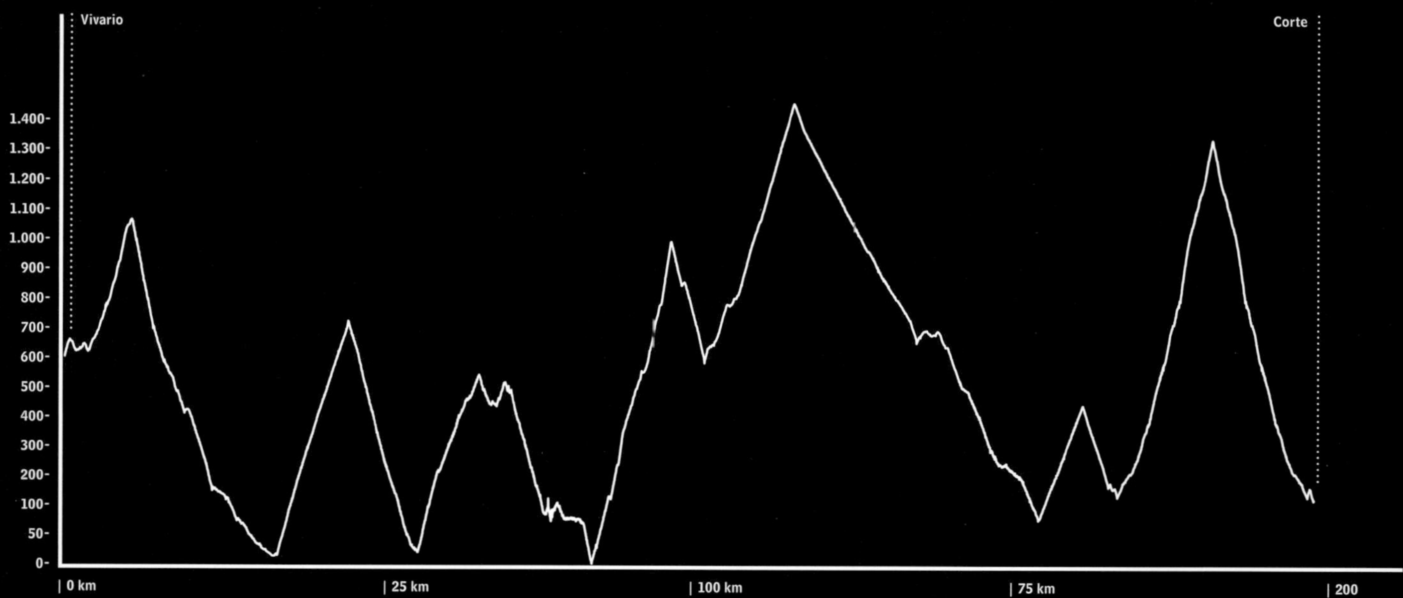

Calvi
Balagne
Filosorma
Niolo
Nebbio
Casinca
Castagniccia
Corte (Corti)
Parc Naturel Régional de la Corse
C O R S E
AJACCIO (AJACCIU)
Golfe d'Ajaccio
TYRRH
Plaine Orientale
Fiumorbo
Col de Vizzavona
Zicavo (Zicavu)
Santa-Maria-Figaniella
Petreto-Bicchisano (Pitretu-Bicchisgia)
Aléria
Bastelica
Evisa

D147

CORTE
BASTIA

207 KM • 4 STUNDEN // 128 MILES • 4 HOURS

Badehose nicht vergessen, die muss heute in der Reisetasche ganz nach oben. Sie hat noch ein paar eingetrocknete Salzränder vom Ausflug ins Meer, aber die werden wir ganz bestimmt los. Wie das in den Bergen funktionieren soll? – Ganz einfach: in einem der kalten Gebirgsbäche Korsikas.

—

Don't forget your swimsuit. In fact, make sure to pack it at the top of your travel bag today. It may still have a few dried salt marks from the last trip to the sea, but they will soon disappear. How is that going to happen in the mountains? – The answer is quite simple: by taking a dip in one of the cold mountain streams of Corsica.

Wenn die Mittelmeersonne zur Mittagszeit streng vom Himmel glüht, zieht einen die erfrischende Kühle der Wasserläufe magisch an. Und zu unserer letzten Etappe auf Korsika passt das feierliche Eintauchen zum Abschied ohnehin ... Während wir darüber nachdenken, packt uns der Blues. Der heißt auf Korsika „Paghjella“, ist ein mehrstimmig-polyphoner Gesang – zumindest steht das so im Reiseführer. Ganz praktisch ist der Paghjella in gesungenen Tönen verpackter Weltschmerz, herzerweichende Klage, spirituelles Lockerwerden. Man muss den korsischen Dialekt überhaupt nicht verstehen, um beim Zuhören nicht sofort zu wissen, um was es geht. Denn nicht nur die gesungenen Worte sind es, die unter die Haut gehen, sondern vor allem deren Transportmittel: Der schwebende, flirrende, sich überlagernde und gegenseitig auflösende, dann wieder anreichernde und verstärkende Sound von Stimmen, die nebeneinander, miteinander, übereinander und gegeneinander Töne treffen. Frequenzen zwischen Chaos und perfekter Präzision. Magisch. Spektakulär. Atemberaubend.

Den Paghjella findet man gern im hallenden Raum von Kirchen. In den Reihen sitzen hypnotisierte Menschen, von roher Emotion stocksteif gefrostet, bis ins Mark ergriffen, während vorne ein Halbrund von Sängern in höchster Konzentration Schallwellen erzeugt. Stimmbänder werden gespannt, häufig halten sich die Sänger ein Ohr zu, um nicht auf den Ton des Nebenmanns gezogen zu werden und um nach der eigenen Frequenz in den Schädelknochen zu tasten. Und rundherum halten Heilige aus Stein und Gold, Jesus und Maria, den Atem an. Schaudern in einer ewig-epischen Gänsehaut. Das ist der Paghjella.

Ein klein wenig fühlt sich so auch der bevorstehende Abschied von der Insel an. Tieftraurig und endgültig, gleichzeitig aber auch dankbar und beschenkt. Eine leicht verzagte Stimme in uns fragt: Was, wenn du nie wieder hierher kommst? Und diese Möglichkeit scheint einem so schlecht auszuhalten, dass man sich mit Kloß im Hals in die Hand verspricht alles zu tun, um dies auf keinen Fall eintreten zu lassen. Wir werden wieder da sein! Und wie! – In dieser feierlichen Stimmung, vollkommen im Jetzt, geht es auf die letzten Kilometer unserer Reise. Beim Hinausfahren aus Corte nehmen wir die Stadt noch einmal so richtig wahr. Die

As the Mediterranean sun blazes harshly at midday, we are drawn as if by magic to the refreshing coolness of the inland water sources. A celebratory plunge is the perfect fit for the last leg of our journey in Corsica... As we think about it, we're enveloped by the spirit of the blues. In Corsica it is called “paghjella”, a multipart, polyphonic song – at least that's what the travel guidebook says. In practical terms, the paghjella is world-weariness packed into songs of heart-rending lamentation and spiritual release. You don't have to understand the Corsican dialect to recognize immediately what you're listening to. After all, it's not just the sung words that get under your skin, but also the way they are expressed: the sounds of human voices float, shimmer, overlap and dissolve, then again enriching and reinforcing one another as they meet in harmony, inhabiting frequencies that waver between chaos and perfect precision. Magical. Spectacular. Simply breathtaking.

The paghjella is often heard in the echoing spaces of churches. People sit in a trance-like state in the pews, frozen to the core by raw emotion, while a semicircle of singers in front of them creates highly concentrated waves of sound. The singers' vocal cords are tense and they often cover their ears to close off the sound of the person next to them and to feel for their own frequency inside their skulls. All around us, saints of stone and gold, Jesus and Mary, hold their breath, shuddering with eternally epic goosebumps. That's what paghjella is all about.

We get a similar feeling when we think about our impending farewell to the island. The prospect seems deeply sad and final, but at the same time we are grateful for the gift we have received. A slightly despondent voice inside us asks: what if you never come back here again? And this possibility seems so hard to bear that, with a lump in your throat, you promise yourself to do everything you can to ensure that this doesn't happen. We will be back! And how! – In this celebratory mood, completely in the here and now, we start the last stage of our journey. As we drive out of Corte, we really take in the city again. The bells in the slender tower of the Chjesa di l'Annunziata ring out a touching farewell. In front of its porch, the statue of General Giovan Pietro Gaffori points vaguely into the distance – you can hardly help feeling that he would actually much rather draw attention to

D147

Glocken im spargeldünnen Turm der Chjesa di l'Annunziata bimmeln ein rührendes Adieu. Vor ihrem Portal deutet die Statue des General Giovan Pietro Gaffori unbestimmt ins Weite – man kann sich kaum des Eindrucks erwehren, dass er eigentlich viel lieber auf die Einschusslöcher an der Fassade der Bar de la Haute Ville hinter sich aufmerksam machen würde. Die stammen von einem alten Scharmützel zwischen korsischen Freiheitskämpfern und französischen Truppen. Wie kaum eine andere korsische Stadt brütet Corte eben immer noch über Korsikas Vergangenheit als Spielball der Mächte von außen, hier ist immer wieder zu spüren, wie wenig sich die Insel bis heute mit einem Schicksal als Provinz italienischer Stadtstaaten oder Frankreichs abgefunden hat. Die Geschichte Cortes, mit ihren kurzen Phasen als Hauptstadt eines unabhängigen Korsika, ist immer noch lebendig, der alte Widerstandsgeist geht argwöhnisch und leicht reizbar in den schmalen Gässchen der Stadt in den Bergen um. Zur Kontrolle des korsischen Selbstbewusstseins haben die Genueser ihre Citadella di Corti gebaut, in der aufkommenden Hitze des Vormittags thront sie als massiger Klotz auf einem Felsplateau über der Stadt und scheint deren Umtriebe immer noch ein klein wenig zu belauern.

Wir fahren nach Norden hinaus, lassen die Stadt zwischen den Berggipfeln zurück und folgen dabei der bekannten Route: vorbei am Toivonen-Crash auf der D18, vorbei an Castirla und dann vorbei am Abzweig der D84, auf der wir am Vortag angekommen sind. Oben bei Popolasca ist die D18 nur noch ein schmales Asphaltband, das sich schüchtern über Almen und durch verwunschene Täler dahinschlängelt, schließlich als letztes Anzeichen von Zivilisation in wilder Macchie dahinzieht. Gegenverkehr haben wir kaum, aber die Ruinen verfallener Gehöfte, Wachtürme oder Kirchlein erzählen davon, dass hier oben im Valle d'Ostia einmal mehr los war. Erst in Ponte Leccia angekommen, endet das magische Gefühl verwaister Einsamkeit – und wir suchen uns schleunigst eine neue Flucht ins Wilde. So schnell wollen wir die Berge nicht verlassen. Im Asco-Tal fahren

the bullet holes on the facade of the Bar de la Haute Ville behind him. They are the last witnesses to an old skirmish between Corsican freedom fighters and French troops.

More than any other Corsican city, Corte still broods over the island's past as a plaything of outside powers. Here you can feel again and again just how little the island has come to terms with its fate as a province of Italian city-states or France. The history of Corte, with its brief spells as the capital of an independent Corsica, is still alive. The old spirit of resistance still haunts the narrow streets of the mountain town, suspicious and hot-headed. The Genoese built their Citadella di Corti in a move designed to quell Corsican self-determination. In the rising heat of the morning, the citadel towers over the city like a massive block on a rocky plateau, seemingly still spying on its all the comings and goings below.

We head north, leaving town between the mountain peaks, following the familiar route: past the site of Toivonen's crash on the D18, past Castirla and then past the junction of the D84, where we arrived the day before. Up at Popolasca, the D18 is just a narrow strip of asphalt that meanders shyly over alpine pastures and through magical valleys, the last sign of civilization in the wild surroundings of the maquis. We meet hardly any oncoming traffic, but the ruins of dilapidated farmsteads, watchtowers or little churches tell us that there was once a lot more going on up here in the Valle d'Ostia. As we arrive in Ponte Leccia, the magical feeling of being all alone comes to an end – and we quickly look for a new escape into the wild.

We don't wish to leave the mountains so soon. In the Asco valley we head west again, weaving our way out of the Mediterranean atmosphere of the valley and climbing further and further up under a crystal-clear mountain sky. Lean-looking pine trees struggle upwards with us. The river meets us at the valley floor, bubbling ice-cold and clear through a rocky bed. After completing a set of resolute switchbacks

RESTAURANT

AUX COQUILLAGES DE DIANA
ETANG DE DIANA
20270 ALÉRIA

wir noch einmal nach Westen, schlängeln uns aus der mediterran wirkenden Gegend im Tal immer weiter hinauf unter einen glasigen Berghimmel. Magere Kiefern mühen sich mit uns hinauf, am Talboden kommt uns der Fluss entgegen, sprudelt eiskalt und klar durch ein felsiges Bett. Nach einem Satz entschlossener Serpentinen zum Finale landen wir am Fuß von kernigen Felswänden. Die Straße endet, nur die Kabel eines kleinen Skilifts führen weiter hinauf, aber allzu weit kann das nicht mehr gehen. Von hier aus ist bereits der Sattel zwischen den Bergwänden am Talende zu sehen.

Auf dem Weg zurück, stehen hinter einer Kehre plötzlich ein paar hellbraune Kühe am Straßenrand, klatschen mit den Schwänzen nach Fliegen und glotzen uns neugierig an. Als wir langsam vorbeirollen, setzen sie sich in Bewegung und führen ein schüchternes Kalb hinter eine Gruppe von Felsen, verschwinden in Richtung des Flusses. Das wirkt wie eine Einladung: An der alten Genueser-Brücke vor Asco stoppen wir, schnappen uns die Badehosen und klettern zum Fluss hinunter.

Unten am Wasser drücken wir uns eine Weile über die mächtigen Geröllbrocken, suchen eine Stelle zum Einstieg – und beschließen am Ende doch den direkten Weg: Luft anhalten und mit einem großen Sprung hinein ins durchsichtig-türkisgrüne Wasser des Asco. Der ist nicht tief, aber es reicht, damit sein bitterkaltes Wasser über dem Kopf zusammenschlägt. Schock. Adern ziehen sich zusammen, nach wenigen Minuten ziehen sich Krämpfe durch die Beine. Raus aus dem Wasser, zum Aufwärmen auf die Felsen. Mit geschlossenen Augen in der Sonne sitzen, den mürben Duft des Wassers einatmen und spüren, wie langsam wieder Leben in die Glieder zieht. Und dann wieder von vorn.

Es dauert lange, bis wir wieder unterwegs sind und uns von der Schwerkraft in das Tal hinunterziehen lassen, den ganzen Weg zurück nach Ponte Lecchia. Von dort geht es dann einfach in die andere Richtung, die Wegweiser in Richtung Bastia auf der zielstrebig dahinmarschierenden T20 ignorieren

before reaching our final destination, we end up at the foot of rugged rock faces. The road ends here with just the cables of a small ski lift continuing on further up for a short while. From here you can already see the saddle between the mountain walls at the end of the valley. On the way back, beyond a hairpin bend, we suddenly encounter a couple of light-brown cows standing on the side of the road, swatting at flies with their tails and staring at us curiously.

As we slowly roll by, they start to move, ushering a shy calf behind a group of rocks, then disappearing towards the river. It feels like an invitation: we stop at the old Genoese bridge in front of Asco, grab our swimsuits and climb down to the river. Down by the water we clamber over the mighty boulders for a while, looking for a place to get in. In the end we decide to take the direct approach: we hold our breath and take the plunge into the transparent, turquoise-green water of the Asco. It's not deep, but it's enough for its bitterly cold water to smash over your head.

Your veins constrict in shock and, after a few minutes, cramps start to run through your legs. We climb out of the water again and onto the rocks to warm up. Sitting in the sun with our eyes closed, we breathe in the mellow scent of the water and feel the life is slowly returning to our limbs again. And then we do it all over again. It takes us a long time to get back on the road, letting gravity take us down the valley all the way back to Ponte Lecchia. From there we continue in the other direction, studiously ignoring the signposts for Bastia on the steadfast T20.

After a few minutes we are almost alone again, twisting and turning in wondrous countryside while the leaves of the plane trees flutter in a warm breeze, the sun brushes the boulders and scrub and a resinous scent emanates from the mountainsides. At some point the approaching slopes of the valley take tight control of the previously free-and-easy landscape, so that the road has to fight its way forward again, carving a slalom path under sweet chestnut trees, while ivy and ferns lend the

D5

Bis Campile geht das so, dann schlagen wir uns in Richtung Bisinchi nach Westen und landen schließlich bei Castello-di-Rostino am Fluss Golo. Hier, bei der Brücke Ponte Novu besiegelte eine französische Armee das Schicksal Korsikas und schlug die korsischen Truppen unter deren Kommandant Pasquale Paoli.

wir geflissentlich. Nach wenigen Minuten sind wir wieder nahezu allein unterwegs, kurven in einem wunderlichen Land dahin, während die Blätter von Platanen in einem warmen Wind wirbeln, die Sonne über Geröll und Gestrüpp streift, ein harziger Duft aus den Berghängen fächelt. Irgendwann nehmen die herandrängenden Talhänge die eben noch freie Landschaft in den Schwitzkasten, jetzt muss sich die Straße wieder vorankämpfen, ackert sich im Slalom unter Kastanienbäumen voran, während Efeu und Farn der Welt einen dunkelgrünen Teint verleihen. Bis Campile geht das so, dann schlagen wir uns in Richtung Bisinchi nach Westen und landen schließlich bei Castello-di-Rostino am Fluss Golo. Hier, bei der Brücke Ponte Novu besiegelte eine französische Armee das Schicksal Korsikas und schlug die korsischen Truppen unter deren Kommandant Pasquale Paoli. Am Gedenkstein ist auch heute noch klar, dass die Korsen diese Angelegenheit mit andauerndem Trotz erinnern: Die Flagge Korsikas mit dem Mohren-Kopf auf weißem Grund ist hier das prägende Element, lässt keinen Deutungsspielraum, wen die Korsen auch heute noch gern als Sieger der Partie sähen.

Wir fahren weiter, die Schnittstelle der Geschichte hat uns an unser eigenes, nahes Schicksal erinnert: Einen Termin, den wir am Abend mit einem Fährschiff in Bastia haben. Auf der D5 kurven wir nach Norden, weiter, immer weiter. Wechseln dann auf die D82, fahren wie in einem Traum, kurz vor dem Aufwachen, wenn man sich noch mit aller Macht festhalten mag. Südlich von Bastia stürzt sich die Straße ans Meer, plötzlich ist alles ganz banal. Die Vororte, die Autos und Motorroller. Dann die Citadelle de Bastia und gleich danach der Hafen. Unser Schwung trägt uns gerade noch auf die Rampe, in den Bauch des Schiffs. Korsika. Avvedeci, du Schöne, Geheimnisvolle.

This continues as far as Campile, when we head west in the direction of Bisinchi and end up at Castello di Rostino on the Golo river. Here, at the Ponte Novu Bridge, a French army sealed the fate of Corsica and defeated the Corsican troops under their commander Pasquale Paoli.

surroundings a dark green complexion. This continues as far as Campile, when we head west in the direction of Bisinchi and end up at Castello di Rostino on the Golo river. Here, at the Ponte Novu Bridge, a French army sealed the fate of Corsica and defeated the Corsican troops under their commander Pasquale Paoli. The memorial stone still makes it clear today that the Corsican remember this matter with constant defiance: the Corsican flag with the Moor's head on a white background is the defining element here, leaving no room for interpretation as to who the Corsicans would still like to see the winner of this particular game.

We drive on. The interface with history has reminded us of our own upcoming fate: an evening appointment with a ferry in Bastia. We curve north on the D5, ever onward. Then we switch to the D82, driving as in a dream. We have reached the point just before waking up, when you try to hold on with all your might. South of Bastia, the road rushes to the sea and, suddenly everything becomes quite banal. The suburbs, the cars and scooters. We encounter the Citadelle de Bastia and then the port. Our momentum just about carries us up the ramp and into the belly of the ship. Avvedeci Corsica, you beautiful, mysterious island.

HOTEL

HÔTEL CASTEL BRANDO
LIEU-DIT
20222 BRANDO
WWW.CASTELBRANDO.COM

CORTE BASTIA

Zum Ziel der Reise in Bastia arbeiten wir uns durchs Gebirge nach Norden: Startend in der ehemaligen Hauptstadt Corte geht es über Castirla und Popolasca bis nach Ponte Leccia, hier fahren wir ins Tal des Asco hinein. Dieser Fluss speist sich aus dem Monte-Cinto-Massiv, sein Tal gehört zusammen mit dem Restonica-Tal weiter südlich zu den landschaftlichen Juwelen des korsischen Hochgebirges. Von der Mündung des Asco in den Gollo bis zum Ende des Tals im Hochgebirge fährt die Straße durch eine ständig wechselnde Landschaft, von beinahe mediterranem Ambiente bis in alpines Terrain. Mit einem Umweg über wilde Kurvenstraßen zwischen Morosaglia und Quercitello und dann weiter zur Abtei von Casablanca geht es in einem weiten Bogen nach Norden, über Campile landen wir schließlich an der Ponte Novu in Castello-di-Rostino. Auch bis nach Murato, Oletta und Barbeggio haben wir noch viele kurvenreiche Kilometer vor uns, erst danach geht es in entspannterem Gelände zurück an die Küste. In Bastia haben wir schließlich die Runde um und über Korsika geschlossen, die Fähre zum Festland wartet bereits.

—

We work our way north through the mountains to the final destination of our trip in Bastia: starting in the former capital of Corte, we pass through Castirla and Popolasca to Ponte Leccia, where we enter the Asco valley. This river flows from the Monte Cinto massif. Its valley, along with the Restonica valley further south, is one of the jewels of the Corsican high mountain landscape. From the point where the Asco flows into the Gollo to the end of the valley in the high mountains, the road bisects a constantly changing landscape, from an almost Mediterranean ambience to alpine terrain. Taking a detour via wild winding roads between Morosaglia and Quercitello and then on to the Abbey of Casablanca, we head north in a wide arc, via Campile and finally end up at the Ponte Novu in Castello-di-Rostino. We still have a long winding road ahead of us to Murato, Oletta and Barbeggio. Only then do we return to the coast and more relaxed terrain. In Bastia we finally complete the circuit around and over Corsica and the ferry to the mainland already awaits.

---

207 KM • 4 STUNDEN // 128 MILES • 4 HOURS

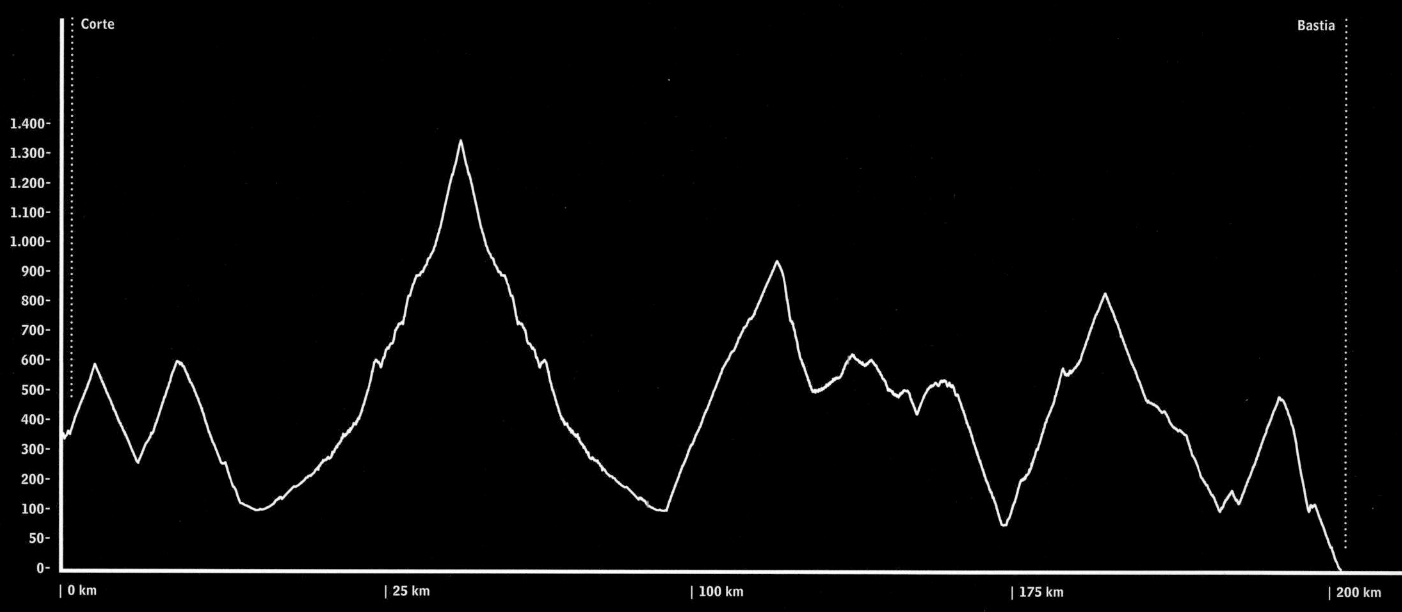

BASTIA
Ville-di-Pietrabugno (E Vile de Petrabugnu)
San-Martino-di-Lota
Saint-Florent (San Fiurenzu)
Golfe de St-Florent
Désert des Agriates
L'Île-Rousse (Isula Rossa)
Calvi
Balagne
Nebbio
Castagniccia
Niolo
Corte (Corti)
Parc Naturel Régional de la Corse
CORSE
Aleria
Plaine Orientale
Fiumorbo
Vivario (Vivariu)
Col de Vizzavona
Bocognano (Bucugnanu)
Nonza
Brando
Cagnano
Canari
Oletta
Biguglia
Borgo (U Borgu)
Ponte-Leccia
Omessa
Morosaglia (Merusaglia)
Asco (Ascu)
Calacuccia
Venaco (Venacu)
Ghisonaccia (Ghjsunaccia)
Ghisoni
Vezzani
Cervione (Cervioni)
Calenzana (Calinzana)
Lumio (Lumiu)
Algajola
Monte Cinto
Monte Rotondo
Carcopino
Tavera
Vero
Ucciani (Ucciani)
Soccia
Letia
Renno
Murzo (Murzu)
Vico (Vicu)
Balogna
Marignana
Evisa
Cristinacce
Azzana
Rosazia (Rusazia)
Salice (U Salice)
Pastricciola
Ambiegna
Arro (Arru)
Casaglione (Casagliu)
Sarrola (Sarrula)
Carbuccia
Tavaco (Tavacu)
Peri
Bastelica
Isolaccio-di-Fiumorbo
Antisanti
Pietroso (U Petrosu)
Muracciole
Noceta
Rospigliani
Casevecchie (E Case Vechje)
Aghione
Linguizzetta
Tox (Tocchisi)
Talasani
Poggio-Mezzana (U Poghju-Mezzana)
Valle-di-Campoloro (E Valle di Campuloru)
San Giuliano (S.Ghjulianu)
Chiatra (Chjatra)
Canale-di-Verde
Vescovato (U Viscuvatu)
Penta-di-Casinca
Lucciana
Pietracorbara (A Petracurbara)
Sisco (Siscu)
Olcani
Ogliastro (Ogliastru)
Luri
Pino (U Pinu)
Morsiglia (Mursigliu)
Tomino (Tuminu)
Meria
Barbaggio (Barbaghju)
Patrimonio (U Patrimoniu)
Farinole (Faringule)
Poggio-d'Oletta (U Poghju d'Oletta)
Murato (Muratu)
Rapale
Vallecalle
Santo-Pietro-di-Tenda (Santu Petru di Tenda)
San-Gavino-di-Tenda (San Gavinu di Tenda)
Sorio (Soriu)
Pieve
Rutali
Urtaca
Lama
Novella (Nuvella)
Palasca
Belgodère (Balgudè)
Occhiatana (Ochjatana)
Costa
Speloncato (Spuncatu)
Nessa (Nesce)
Feliceto (Filicetu)
Muro (Muru)
Avapessa
Cateri
Aregno
Lavatoggio (U Lavatoghju)
Corbara (Curbara)
Santa-Reparata-di-Balagna
Monticello (U Monticellu)
Sant'Antonino (Sant'Antoninu)
Pigna
Montegrosso
Zilia
Moncale (U Mucale)
Pioggiola
Olmi-Cappella (Olmi è Capella)
Mausoleo (Musuleu)
Vallica
Castifao
Moltifao (Moltifau)
Piedigriggio (Pedigrisgiu)
Popolasca
Castiglione
Prato-di-Giovellina
Gavignano (Gavignanu)
Castineta
Saliceto (U Salicetu)
Alti
Lano (Lanu)
Sermano (Sermanu)
Bustanico (Bustanicu)
Cambia
Rusio (Rusiu)
Tralonca
Soveria
Castirla
Lozzi
Corscia
Casamaccioli
Albertacce
Santa-Lucia-di-Mercurio (Sta Lucia di Mercuriu)
Favalello
Mazzola
Sant'Andréa-di-Bozio
Erbajolo
Focicchia
Altiani
Piedicorte-di-Gaggio
Pietraserena
Zuani
Ampriani
Zalana
Matra
Moïta
Pancheraccia
Tallone
Pianello
Campi
Piazzali
Novale
Pietra-di-Verde (A Petra di Verde)
Ortale
Perelli (I Perelli)
Sant'Andréa-di-Cotone
Felce
Tarrano (Tarranu)
Carpineto
Stazzona
Piedipartino
Carcheto-Brustico
Pietricaggio (Petricaghju)
Piobetta
Valle-d'Orezza
Monacia-d'Orezza
Piazzole
Verdèse
Rapaggio
Polveroso
Nocario
Campana
Piedicroce
Croce
Ficaja
Piccolo
Quercitello
Porta
La Porta
San-Damiano (San Damianu)
San-Gavino-d'Ampugnani
Pruno (Prunu)
Velone-Orneto (Vilone-Ornetu)
San Giovanni-di-Moriani (S.Ghjuvanni di Moriani)
Santa-Lucia-di-Moriani
Sta-Reparata-di-Moriani
San Nicolao (S.Niculaiu)
Taglio-Isolaccio (Tagliu-Isulacciu)
Castellare-di-Casinca
Sorbo-Ocagnano
Venzolasca (A Venzulasca)
Loreto-di-Casinca
Silvareccio
Casabianca
Poggio-Marinaccio
Casalta
Monte
Olmo (L'Olmu)
Prunelli-di-Casacconi
Campile
Bisinchi
Crocicchia
Ortiporio
Penta-Acquatella
Castello-di-Rostino
Valle-di-Rostino (E Valle di Rustinu)
Gavignano
Lento (Lentu)
Bigorno (Bigornu)
Canavaggia (A Canavaghja)
Campitello (U Campitellu)
Scolca (A Scolca)
Volpajola (A Vulpajola)
Vignale
Olmeta-di-Tuda
Olmeta-di-Capocorso (Olmeta di Capicorsu)
Santa-Maria-di-Lota
Pietrabugno
Oletta
Furiani
Pietralba (Petralba)
Casanova (A Casa Nova)
Riventosa
Poggio-di-Venaco (U Poghju di Venacu)
Santo Pietro-di-Venaco (Santu Petru di Venacu)
Orto (Ortu)
Poggiolo (U Poghjolu)
Guagno (Guagnu)
Arbori (Arburi)
Lopigna
Cannelle (E Cannelle)
San-Andrea-d'Orcino (Sant'Andria d'Orcinu)
Calcatoggio (Calcatoghju)
Appietto (Appiettu)
Sari-d'Orcino (Sari d'Orcinu)
Poggio-di-Nazza (U Poghju di Nazza)
Lugo-di-Nazza (U Lucu di Nazza)
Prunelli-di-Fiumorbo
Serra-di-Fiumorbo
Manso (Mansu)
Filosorma
Forêt Domaniale du Fango
Forêt de Perticatu
Ota
Col de Sevi
Col de Vergio
Réserve Naturelle de l'Étang de Biguglia
Étang de Biguglia
Domaine de Casabianda
70
19
28
22
47
51
75

WAVES

ASK THE LOCAL

Mein Name ist William, ich bin 26 Jahre alt und auch als Pinchuledu bekannt. Ich bin derzeit im französischen Militär und Fotograf. Mein erster Kontakt mit Autos waren die Erzählungen meiner Mutter über Rallyefahrten mit ihrem Renault R8 Gordini. Als ich Metzger wurde, war ich den Pariser Sternerestaurants näher als der Straße. Aber schließlich wurde ich Botschafter des Husqvarna France Teams und interessierte mich etwas mehr für die Fotografie. Ich hatte das Glück und konnte mich einige Jahre dem Motorradfahren widmen, was mir auch die Möglichkeit gab, den Lebensstil rund um Motorräder, Autos und Fotografie kennenzulernen. Heute lebe ich vor allem von meiner Leidenschaft für die Fotografie in Kombination mit Autos. Korsika-Rundfahrten, Sonntagsausflüge, Roadtrips durch die Dolomiten, Track Days ... das waren in den letzten drei Jahren meine Lieblingsbeschäftigungen.

–

My name is William, I'm 26 years old and I am also known as Pinchuledu. I am currently serving in the French military and a photographer. My earliest contact with cars came from listening to my mother's stories about rallying in her Renault R8 Gordini. When I became a butcher, my life was more about Michelin-starred restaurants of Paris than the open road. But I ended up joining the Husqvarna France team as an ambassador and became a bit more interested in photography. I was lucky enough to devote a number of years to motorcycling, which also gave me the chance to experience life around motorbikes, cars and photography. These days I basically earn a living from my passion for photography combined with cars. Between Tours de Corse, Sunday rides, road trips through the Dolomites, track days... This has been my favorite activity for the last three years.

Warum hat sich Korsika nie so richtig an Frankreich, Italien oder ein anderes Land angepasst? Korsika war schon immer schwer zu beugen. Im Jahr 1755 führte Pasquale Paoli Korsika in die Unabhängigkeit und gab der Insel eine Verfassung, womit Korsika die erste Region der Welt mit einem modernen demokratischen Staat wurde. Genua trat Korsika im Jahr 1768 an Frankreich ab und beendete damit die Unabhängigkeit der Insel. Es folgten zwei große Kämpfe zwischen den Franzosen und den Korsen unter der Führung von Pasquale Paoli. 1976 erhob sich eine Minderheit der korsischen Bevölkerung gegen den französischen Staat wegen der ungerechten Umverteilung von Reichtümern an die algerische Bevölkerung im Exil, was zu einem „radikalen" korsischen Nationalismus und zu 38 Jahren bewaffneten Kampfes führte.

Auf die Gefahr hin, einen Fehler zu begehen: Warum sollte Korsika um jeden Preis französisch bleiben? Für Korsika ist die Unterstützung der französischen Regierung unerlässlich. Der Tourismus und die lokale Wirtschaft reichen nicht aus, um das ganze Jahr über ein gutes Auskommen zu ermöglichen. Korsika lebt von den Subventionen, dem Wissen und den Mitteln, die der französische Staat der Insel zur Verfügung stellt. Korsika hat es dank seiner Insellage und seiner strengen Regeln geschafft, als Collectivité Territoriale zu gelten, und verfügt seit 1982 über ein eigenes Parlament und einige für Korsika spezifische Gesetze, insbesondere ein Steuergesetz, das auf das Jahr 1800 unter dem Konsulat von Napoleon Bonaparte zurückgeht.

Welche drei Dinge sind „typisch korsisch"? - *Charcuterie* bzw. Fleischprodukte vom korsischen Schwein (porcu nustrale), das sich hauptsächlich von dem ernährt, was es in der Macchia findet, nämlich von Kastanien, die in der korsischen Machja reichlich vorhanden sind und ihm einen unnachahmlichen Geschmack verleihen. - *L'Immortelle* (die italienische Strohblume), eine auf Korsika sehr verbreitete Pflanze mit einem unverwechselbaren Duft. Sie wird gesammelt, verarbeitet und in vielen Bereichen verwendet. Seit dem Altertum ist sie als Pflanze mit vielen Tugenden und auch als Heilpflanze bekannt. - *Die Flüsse.* Wenn man von Korsika spricht, denkt man zuerst an atemberaubende Strände mit kristallklarem Wasser, feinem und heißem Sand und zahlreichen Meerestieren. Aber Korsika hat auch seine Flüsse, die eine Oase der Ruhe und Entspannung sind. Dort finden Sie im Hochsommer abseits der Menschenmassen Ruhe und vor allem Abkühlung.

Welche drei Orte müssen in einem Werbefilm über Korsika unbedingt dabei sein? Bavella, Piana und Bonifacio: der schönste Berg mit seiner rosafarbenen Granitlandschaft, ein UNESCO-Weltkulturerbe und eine mittelalterliche Stadt mit außergewöhnlichen Baudenkmälern.

Why has Corsica never really made a good fit with France or Italy or anywhere else? Corsica has always been strong-willed. In 1755, Pasquale Paoli led the island to independence and established a constitution, making Corsica the first region in the world to form a modern democratic state. In 1768, Genoa ceded Corsica to France, putting an end to its independence. Two major battles ensued between the French and the Corsicans led by Pasquale Paoli. In 1976, a minority of Corsicans rose up against the French state due to the perceived unfair redistribution of wealth to exiled Algerians, giving rise to "radical" Corsican nationalism and 38 years of armed struggle.

And at the risk of offending, why should Corsica remain French at all costs? French government support for Corsica is essential. Tourism and the local economy are not enough to provide a comfortable year-round living, and Corsica survives through the subsidies, expertise and resources that the French state makes available to the island. Thanks to its island status and its strict adherence to regulations, Corsica is considered a Collectivité Territoriale, and, since 1982, has benefited from its own assembly and certain laws specific to Corsica, notably a tax status law dating back to 1800 under Napoleon Bonaparte's Consulate.

Name three things that are "typically Corsican"? - *Corsican charcuterie* or pork products made from the meat of local pigs (porcu nustrale), which feed mainly on what they find in the scrubland, especially sweet chestnuts, which grow abundantly in the Corsican maquis, giving it an unmistakable flavor. - *L'Immortelle* (a muredda), a plant with a distinctive fragrance that is found all over in Corsica. It is harvested, processed and used for many purposes. Since ancient times, it has been recognized as a plant with many virtues, including medicinal properties. - *The rivers.* When you talk about Corsica, you first think about breathtaking beaches with crystal-clear water, fine, hot sand and rich marine life. But Corsica also has its rivers, which are a haven of peace and quiet away from the crowds on the coast in midsummer, and above all, a source of coolness. And don't worry, there's plenty to please the eye too: there is hiking, breathtaking scenery, natural swimming pools, canyoning... The rivers really are a must and you'll also find pristine water there too.

If you were making a promotional film about Corsica, which three places would you include? Bavella, Piana and Bonifacio: the most scenic mountain with its pink granite scenery, a UNESCO World Heritage Site, and a medieval city with exceptional heritage.

If you could choose three stages for the next Corsica Rally, which sections of the route would you drive?

Du kannst drei Etappen für die nächste Rallye Korsika auswählen. Auf welchen Abschnitten der Strecke fährst du? Ich fahre definitiv den Col de Sorba, den Col de Saint-Eustache und den Col de Bacinu.

Wenn du nicht nach Korsika zurückkehren könntest, in welche Länder würdest du gehen, weil sie dir zumindest ein bisschen korsisches Gefühl vermitteln? Ich würde ins französische Baskenland gehen. Ich habe dort einige Monate gelebt und sowohl das Baskenland als auch Korsika sind von Bergen, Herden und Hirten geprägt. Wunderschöne Gegenden, reich an guten Produkten, althergebrachtem Know-how, schönen, kurvenreichen Straßen und einer Mentalität, die der korsischen sehr ähnlich ist.

Reisen auf Korsika: Welche Jahreszeit ist die beste? Zum Fahren: April, Mai, Juni und September, Oktober. Dazwischen besteht die Gefahr, dass in den Bergen schlechtes Wetter herrscht oder zu viele Touristen unterwegs sind.

Gestrandet auf Korsika: Welche drei Dinge sollte man unbedingt dabei haben? Ein Messer. Ja, die Korsen und ihre Waffen, das ist eine wahre Liebesgeschichte. Einen Käse. Wie kann man ohne ihn überleben? Eine Kamera. Um die Momente zu verewigen, in denen man sich auf Korsika verirrt und die wahre Schönheit dieser Insel entdeckt.

Welchem Prominenten würden Sie gerne Korsika zeigen? Ich würde Korsika gerne dem (Kreativdirektor und Fotografen) Laurent Nivalle zeigen, mit einem 964 Targa oder einem ST 2.5.

Welche drei kulinarischen Spezialitäten Korsikas sollten Besucher unbedingt probieren? Merizani, eine Aubergine, die mit Brot und Brocciu (ein Käse) gefüllt ist. Cannelloni au brocciu oder Canelloni mit Tomatensauce, Brocciu und Spinat. Veau aux olives, Kalbsragout mit Oliven, das normalerweise mit Nudeln serviert wird.

Und welche Lebensmittel, Aktivitäten oder Verhaltensweisen sollte man auf Korsika unbedingt vermeiden? Vermeiden Sie italienisches Essen, korsisches Essen ist besser. Schwimmen Sie nicht im Lac de l'Ospedale. Grüßen Sie, wenn Sie jemandem begegnen, vor allem mitten im Nirgendwo: Das könnte Ihr Rettungsweg zurück in die Stadt sein. Fahren Sie nicht in der Mitte der Fahrbahn. Geben Sie Vollgas und vergessen Sie nicht, sich zu amüsieren.

Welches Land/welche Region der Welt möchtest du besuchen? Welches Abenteuer würdest du gern erleben? Japan! Um das Essen und einen kompletten Tapetenwechsel zu erleben.

Wenn du Korsika für immer verlassen müsstest – wohin würdest du gehen? Nach Österreich oder Südtirol.

I would definitely go for Col de Sorba, Col de Saint-Eustache and Col de Bacinu.

If you could never return to Corsica, where would you choose for at least a little bit of Corsican feeling? I would choose the French Basque country, I lived there for a few months and both the Basque country and Corsica are characterized by mountains, herds of sheep and goats and shepherds. It is a beautiful territory, rich in good produce, ancestral wisdom, beautiful twisty roads and a mindset very similar to the Corsican one.

Which season is the best for traveling in Corsica? For driving, I'd say April, May, June and September, October. Outside those months, there is the danger of bad weather in the mountains or too many tourists.

If you got stranded in Corsica, what are the three things you should definitely have with you? A knife. Yes, the Corsicans and weapons, it's a true love story. Cheese. How could you survive without it? A camera. To capture those moments when you get lost in Corsica and discover the true beauty of this island.

Which celebrity would you like to show around Corsica? I would love to introduce Corsica to (creative director and photographer) Laurent Nivalle in a 964 Targa or an ST 2.5.

Which three culinary specialties of Corsica should visitors try? Merizani, eggplant stuffed with its flesh mixed with bread and Brocciu (a kind of cheese). Cannelloni au brocciu, cannelloni with tomato sauce, brocciu and spinach. Veau aux olives, veal ragout with olives, usually served with pasta.

And what foods or activities or behavior should be absolutely avoided in Corsica? Avoid Italian food, Corsican food is better. Don't swim in the lac de l'Ospedale. Say hello when you pass someone, especially in the middle of nowhere: they could be your lifeline back to the city. Don't drive in the middle of the road. Play hard and don't forget to enjoy yourself.

Which country/region in the world would you most like to visit? What adventures would you like to experience there? Japan! In order to experience the food and a complete change of scenery.

If you had to leave Corsica forever – where would you choose? Austria, South Tyrol.

RISQUE
DE VERGLAS

EG-153-TF

BAC KST AGE

Korsika, das ist mediterraner Raum für Fortgeschrittene. Kein einfaches Land, nicht auf den ersten Blick zu verstehen. Einerseits abgeschieden, andererseits ein integraler Bestandteil der alten Kulturlandschaft des Mittelmeers. Als Insel von einem immerwährend anderen Stern, aber gleichzeitig auch mittendrin im Zentrum der Geschichte Europas. Die schroffe Natur Korsikas und die kantige, trotzige Kultur der Korsen sind kein Stoff für Mainstream-Tourismus im leichtgängigen Rhythmus der All-you-can-eat-Resorts und ewig sonnigen Strandkultur. Dass Korsika sozusagen ein Gebirge im Meer ist, macht eine Erkundung zum kraftraubenden Erlebnis. Dass die Kultur immer eine Art doppelten Boden hat, sich aus unzähligen übereinanderliegenden und verschmolzenen Schichten speist, lässt einen anspruchsvollen Charakter entstehen. Natürlich: Kultur und ist immer und überall kein zusammenhangloses Ereignis – Korsika lässt einen das aber unmissverständlich spüren.

All diese Komplexitäten und Sperrigkeiten waren für uns natürlich Grund genug, die Reise über und um Korsika anzutreten. CURVES ist schließlich keine Gerade, bei uns fährt gelegentlich schon auch die Spucktüte mit. Wir sehen Berge, die sich uns in den Weg stellen, nicht als Hinderungsgrund einer Reise, sondern als ihren eigentlichen Anziehungspunkt. Straßen, die sich in hartem Terrain mühen und schinden, sind uns nicht lästig, sondern Motivation für einen Besuch. Dabei lässt sich dann oft

Corsica is like the Mediterranean on steroids. It is not an easy country to understand at first glance. On the one hand it is quiet and sleepy, while on the other it is an integral part of the ancient cultural landscape of the Mediterranean. It is like an island from a completely different planet, but at the same time is slap bang in the middle of the history of Europe.

Corsica's rugged nature and the island's edgy, defiant culture are not the stuff of mainstream tourism found in easy-going rhythm of all-you-can-eat resorts and perpetually sunny beach culture. The fact that Corsica is actually a mountain range in the sea makes exploring an exhausting experience. The fact that its culture is always a fusion of countless superimposed layers gives rise to a sophisticated character. Of course, culture is always a mix of elements, not a completely standalone phenomenon, and Corsica leaves you in no doubt of this.

Naturally, all of these complexities and difficulties were reason enough for us to choose this journey around Corsica. After all, CURVES isn't about straight lines and sometimes motion sickness can catch us up. We regard the mountains that stand in our way as an actual attraction, rather than an obstacle to our journey. Roads that demand hard work in difficult terrain never put us off, but in fact encourage us to visit. It is often the case that a country's real attractions can only be reached via CURVES.

953
Roughroads
PORSCHE
S PR 9408

feststellen, dass die eigentlichen Attraktionen eines Landes oft nur über CURVES zu erreichen sind. Zugegeben: Manchmal liegt zwischen uns und dem Guten, Schönen und Kostbaren auch einfach nur ein kleiner Spaziergang, und ja, man kommt sogar über die Autobahn hin. Aber das sind Ausnahmen, die die Regel bestätigen: CURVES führen ins Glück. Hinzu kommt, dass bereits das Fahren und Unterwegssein auf diesen mühsamen und wenig ausgetretenen Wegen bereits Ankommen ist. Übrigens, Reisetipp: Korsikas goldene Zeiten sind Ende April und Anfang Mai, dann ist der Schnee in den Bergen verschwunden und die Touristen noch nicht aufgetaucht. Ende September und Anfang Oktober ist es genau andersrum und deshalb genauso gut. Was Korsika zur Empfehlung für Einsteiger macht, die den CURVES-Groove einmal härter erleben wollen, quasi von der geführten Wanderung auf den Klettersteig umsatteln, ist die Tatsache, dass die Insel ausgesprochen gut erreichbar ist: Der Hafen von Bastia liegt nur wenige Fährstunden von den großen Mittelmeer-Häfen Italiens und Frankreichs entfernt. Und angekommen auf Korsika geht es sofort in die Vollen, die Show steigt unmittelbar. Bereits die Küstenstraße rund ums Cap Corse, die fingerartige Halbinsel im Norden, taugt perfekt zum Warmwerden: Anrührend schöne Landschaft plus verrückte Straßen gleich maximale Fahrfreude. Danach zieht es einen an der Westseite regelrecht sogartig bis in den Süden hinunter – und wer dann nicht bereit ist für die Fahrt durchs Gebirge, kann keine Seele haben.

Aber zurück zu unserer Fahrt: Irgendwo unterwegs haben wir einen ersten emotionalen Kassensturz gemacht, quasi nachgesehen, wie hoch der Input des Fahrens ist und wie sich der zum Begeisterungsgrad verhält. Auf manchen Reisen ist das nicht so leicht zu beantworten, auf Korsika war das ein Selbstläufer: hohe Investition in Sachen Schweiß – die Inselstraßen wollen von wachen Geistern mit Kurven-Killerinstinkt niedergekämpft werden –, gleichzeitig aber überbordend hoher Payback. Korsika gibt seine Schönheit und wilden Geist überaus großzügig. Beim Rekapitulieren im CURVES-Team rutschte die Korsika-Tour auf unserer Bestenliste unaufhaltsam immer weiter nach vorn. Die Gründe dafür? – Auch die sind nicht einfach zu benennen. Oder doch? Wir haben folgende Erkenntnis gewonnen: Korsikas Reiz liegt in einer unverstellten Ehrlichkeit. Das Land, die Menschen, die Kultur und das Essen sind unverkünstelt, erdig, sättigend. Dass wir die korsische Küche zur Erklärung herbeiholen, ist übrigens kein Zufall. Unsere Definition Korsikas kam beim Essen zustande, die korsische Küche war unsere Ausgangs-Analogie. Sie ist ehrlich und liebevoll, einfach und gleichzeitig raffiniert. Man spürt ihr eine Herkunft in der Tradition der Toskana ab, meint immer einen Hauch Italiens wahrnehmen zu können, gleichzeitig sind da aber auch die vielen Momente, bei denen der Gaumen innerhalb weniger Augenblicke eine Rundfahrt um das gesamte Mittelmeer antritt. Gewürze, Düfte, Geschmäcker – da ist der Orient, Griechenland, Spanien und Frankreich am Start. Und auch ganz allein Korsika. Die halbwilden Schweine

Admittedly, sometimes it takes just a short walk to reach the most beautiful and precious experiences, and yes, you can often even get there using the highway. But these are the exceptions that prove the rule: following the CURVES route is a sure-fire trip to happiness. In addition, navigating these difficult and little-used trails is a sign that you have arrived. By the way, here's a travel tip: Corsica's golden days are late April and early May, when the snow has disappeared from the mountains and the tourists have not yet appeared. At the end of September and beginning of October, things are exactly the other way around and therefore just as good.

What makes Corsica a good bet for novices who want to experience some tougher CURVES grooves, something like switching from a guided hike to a free climb, is the fact that the island is extremely easy to reach: the port of Bastia is only a few hours by ferry from the major Mediterranean ports in Italy and France. Also, when you arrive in Corsica, the show begins almost immediately. The coastal road around Cap Corse, the finger-like peninsula in the north, is ideal for warming up: heart-stoppingly beautiful scenery plus crazy roads make for maximum driving pleasure. After that, the west coast will draw you all the way down south – and if you're not ready for the drive through the mountains, then you're a lost cause.

But back to our trip: somewhere along the way we made a first emotional "stocktake", so to speak, to determine the input demanded from the driver and how this relates to the level of thrills involved. On some trips that is not an easy question to answer, but on Corsica it was obvious: a high degree of concentration is required – the island roads call for alert minds with a killer instinct for curves – but at the same time the payback is enormous. Corsica is exceedingly generous with its beauty and wild spirit. When reviewing the Corsica tour with the CURVES team, we found it inexorably moving further and further up our list of the best. The reasons? – It isn't easy to explain. Or is it?

We have gained to the following insight: Corsica's appeal lies in its absolute honesty. The country, the people, the culture and the food are unsophisticated, earthy and substantial. By the way, we have good reason for using Corsican cuisine as part of our explanation. We learned to define Corsica through its food, so Corsican cuisine became our initial analogy. It is honest and lovable, simple and sophisticated at the same time. You can sense its origins in the traditions of Tuscany. Although you always think you can identify a touch of Italy, at the same time there are also many moments in which the palate embarks on a tour of the entire Mediterranean in a matter of seconds. The spices, scents and flavors are reminiscent of the Orient, Greece, Spain and France to begin with. But they are also completely and absolutely Corsican. The semi-wild pigs

ESSO
Eminence
Eminence
Eminence
FACOM

und Wildschweine Korsikas – der Übergang kann beinahe fließend sein – dürfen zu ihrem großen Leidwesen als Hauptbestandteil der korsischen Küche gelten. Nummer zwei: der korsische Käse, der es durch seine unübertroffene olfaktorische Würzigkeit (man könnte auch sagen: er stinkt bestialisch) als Hauptdarsteller bis in einen Asterix-Comic geschafft hat. Und Nummer drei: die Kastanie. Kastanienmehl ist auf Korsika die Grundlage köstlicher Gebäcksorten, wird aber sogar auch beim Bierbrauen verwendet.

All das ist so unmissverständlich und eindeutig wie die Insel selbst. Wir sind einen Moment lang wirklich zu Korsen geworden. Korsika hat sich in uns einen Platz gesucht und sich dort eingenistet, wir werden es wohl nicht mehr losbekommen – und wollen das auch nicht. Stattdessen sei hiermit das Kleingedruckte dieser CURVES-Ausgabe ganz groß gedruckt: Wir würden Sie gern zu Korsika verführen, zu Co-Abhängigen dieser Insel machen. Von Einsteigern zu Fortgeschrittenen. Dass wir uns für unsere Fahrten großartige Verbündete suchen, wissen CURVES-Kenner: Wir sind beschenkt mit einer Community, auf deren Wissen und Begeisterung wir auch in Korsika zurückgreifen konnten. Viele Straßen, Punkte, Restaurants oder Hotels hätten wir ohne die Tipps von korsischen CURVES-Fans niemals entdeckt – wir sagen Danke dafür! Und dass die Fahrt zu einem unvergesslichen Moment wurde, liegt am Spirit der wunderbaren Menschen, die dabei waren, egal ob am Steuer, hinter Film- und Fotolinsen, an der Schreibtastatur oder anfeuernd von zu Hause. Und nicht zuletzt hatten wir zwei automobile Glanzstücke dabei, die zu Korsika passen wie Fäuste auf Augen: den Porsche 718 Boxster GTS, ein Kurvensuchgerät par excellence, und den einzigartigen Porsche 911 Dakar.

Die Fähigkeiten dieses Autos, wenn Straßen hart und bitter werden, sich am Ende sogar ganz auflösen, sind unbestechlich und beeindruckend. Wie ein Derwisch turnt er über die kleinsten Sträßchen, bewegt sich mit Biss und Geschmeidigkeit, verbindet Präzision mit Gutmütigkeit. Asphalt, der jedes andere Auto dieser Leistungskategorie in Stücke prügeln würde, nimmt der 911 Dakar mit Großmut und Verbindlichkeit, den bringt so schnell nichts aus der Ruhe. Natürlich haben wir ihn dann immer wagemutiger und vertrauter selbst die kleinen Eselspfade am Ende der Gebirgstäler hinaufgeprügelt oder beim Fotografieren einfach mal über Almen, Schotterstraßen und Nicht-Straßen abgekürzt – der 911 Dakar klettert mit seinem kurzen Radstand, der ebenso hohen wie zusätzlich auf Niveau „Bergziege“ verstellbaren Bodenfreiheit völlig unbarmherzig. Als wir ihn am Ende der Fahrt in seinen Stall bei Porsche Deutschland (Danke! Danke! Danke!) zurückbringen mussten, waren wir diesem Tausendsassa mit Haut und Haaren verfallen. Er ist kein Modeartikel, kein abseitiges Derivat, sondern eine lebende Legende, ein ganz großer Wurf. Aus seinem Cockpit sagen wir: Avvedeci, Korsika. Bis wir uns wiedersehen.

and wild boars of Corsica – it is hard to know where one species ends and the other begins – can be considered the main ingredient of Corsican cuisine. Number two: Corsican cheese, which has made it into an Asterix comic as a leading actor thanks to its unsurpassed olfactory spiciness (one could also say: it stinks like a beast). And number three: the sweet chestnut. Sweet chestnut flour is the basis of delicious pastries in Corsica, but it is also used in beer brewing.

All of this is as unequivocal and clear as the island itself. We really became Corsican for a short time. Corsica has found a place in our hearts that we probably won't be able to get rid of – not that we would want to anyway. Instead, this issue of CURVES is nailing its colors to the mast: our aim is to seduce you to visit Corsica and to make you co-dependent on this island, whether you are CURVES novice or a long-established reader.

CURVES connoisseurs know that we are always looking for great companions on our journeys: we are lucky enough to have a community with knowledge and enthusiasm we could rely on in Corsica. We would never have discovered many roads, waypoints, restaurants or hotels without tips from our Corsican CURVES fans – and for that we thank you! The fact that the drive became an unforgettable experience is due to the spirit of the wonderful people we had with us, whether behind the wheel, behind the cameras, at the keyboard or cheering from home. And last but not least, we had two true automotive jewels with us that were the perfect fit for Corsica: the Porsche 718 Boxster GTS, a cornering specialist par excellence, and the unique Porsche 911 Dakar.

The capabilities of this car when the going gets tough and bitter, or even when the roads dissolve completely into nothingness at the end are undeniably impressive. The car whirled like a dervish through the narrowest streets, moving with astringency and suppleness and combining precision with positive good nature. The 911 Dakar takes asphalt that would smash any other car in this performance category to pieces generously in its stride. Of course we forced the car to climb the narrow donkey tracks at the end of the mountain valleys with increasing daring and confidence. We also took shortcuts across alpine pastures, gravel roads and non-roads, chasing the ideal photograph. The short wheelbase of the Porsche 911 Dakar, as well as its adjustable ground clearance, enabled the car to climb with a nimbleness akin to that of a mountain goat. When we had to return the Porsche 911 Dakar to its home at Porsche Germany (thank you! thank you! thank you!) at the end of the trip, we were completely smitten with this jack of all trades. This is not a fashion item, or some quirky derivative, but rather a living legend and a huge success. From behind the wheel we say: Avvedeci, Corsica. We'll see you again.

S PR 9408

MICHELIN
PRIX IMPOSÉ
KLG

953
Roughroads
S PR 9408

TARR
LE REBELLE
C. MOLITERNI
J. BROCAL REMOHI
LE SABLIER D'OR

CAFÉ
CORSICA
1934

S PR 9408

corsica ferries 10
corsica ferries 11
corsica ferries 12
corsica ferries 15
corsica ferries 16
corsica ferries 17

Exception du Maquis lait cru brebis

953
Roughroads
PORSCHE

S PR 9408

Smile
IF YOU
LIKE ME

14:13
Irgendwas ist schiefgelaufen
Zurück

953
Roughroads

PALAZZU

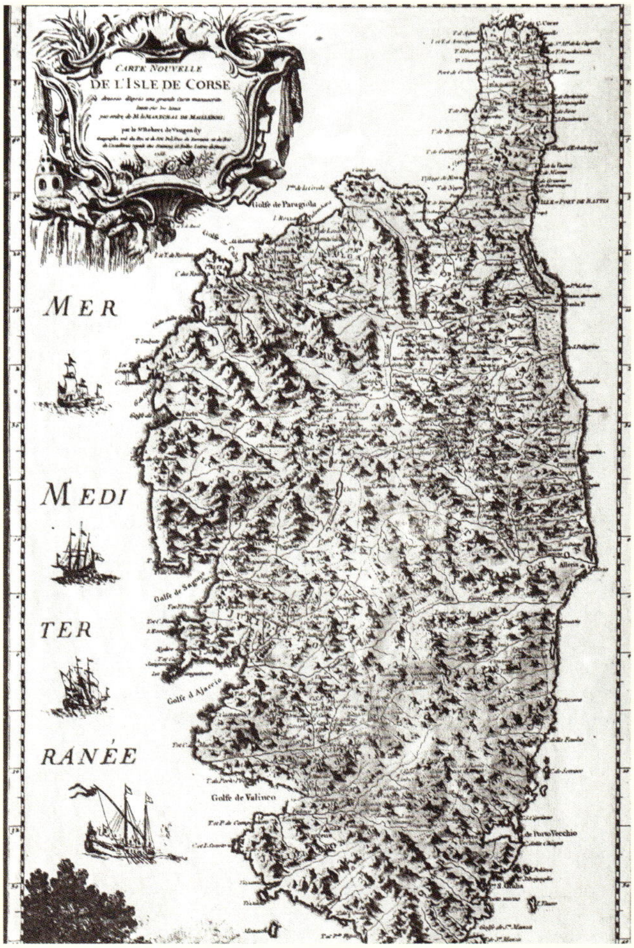
CARTE NOUVELLE
DE L'ISLE DE CORSE
MER
MEDI
TER
RANÉE
Golfe de Valinco

CORSE HELICOPTERE
Helicopter Airline

Roughroads
PORSCHE
953

ATTENTION DANGER
DANGER !
DAM AND POWER STATION:
RISK OF SUDDEN FLOODING
EVEN IN GOOD WEATHER
ACHTUNG,
GEFAHR !
STAUDÄMME
UND KRAFTWERKE:
RASCH ANSTEIGENDES
HOCHWASSER MÖGLICH
SOGAR BEI SCHÖNEM
WETTER
DANGER !
BARRAGES ET CENTRALES:
RISQUE DE MONTÉE SOUDAINE DES EAUX, MÊME PAR BEAU TEMPS
Barrage de CORSCIA
PECHEURS - ATTENTION - DANGER

Bicchisano

PORSCHE
S·PR 9408
Roughroads
PORSCHE
953

953
Roughroads
PORSCHE

PORSCHE
718 Boxster GTS

A vol d'oiseau...
NONZA
bastia 130 KM
CALVI 122 KM
Gualdariccìu 22 KM
43 KM Chisà
Porto Vecchio
62 KM AJACCIO
Corte 87 KM
160 KM CENTURI
20 KM BONIFACIO

Roughroads
PORSCHE
953

953
Roughroads
PORSCHE

AQUAMAN
IN CORSE
DENTI
VS
AQUAMAN

GENDARMERIE NATIONALE
BRIGADE DE PIANA

BOSCH

S PR 9408

953
Roughroads
PORSCHE

Roughroads
PORSCHE
953
S PR 9408

DUNLOP

DANK AN / THANKS TO
Bastian Schramm, Maximilian Ramisch, Philipp Heitsch, Felix Körbel, Ben Winter, Hanno Vienken, Michael Dorn, Michaela Bogner

SPECIAL FX / SPECIAL FX
William (Pinchu at Instagram), AOT Travel - Christian Preiherr, Yannik & Sophie, Anne & Uli (914/6), Frank Wörner, Corse Helicopter, Stephan Volk & Leica, Fabian Isensee

CURVES TRAVEL AGENT:
AOT Travel • info@aottravel.de • Tel. +49 89 12 24 800

ROUTE AS GPX FILE:

Porsche 718 Boxster GTS:
Kraftstoffverbrauch kombiniert: 10,9 – 10,1 l/100 km (WLTP);
CO_2-Emissionen kombiniert: 247 – 230 g/km (WLTP); Stand 06/2023

Fuel consumption combined: 10.9 – 10.1 l/100 km (WLTP);
CO_2 emissions combined: 247 – 230 g/km (WLTP); Status 06/2023

Porsche 911 Dakar:
Fuel consumption combined: 11.3 l/100 km (WLTP);
CO_2 emissions combined: 256 g/km (WLTP); Status 06/2023

Kraftstoffverbrauch kombiniert: 11,3 l/100 km (WLTP);
CO_2-Emissionen kombiniert: 256 g/km (WLTP); Stand 06/2023

IMPRESSUM / IMPRINT

HERAUSGEBER/
PUBLISHER: CURVES MAGAZIN
THIERSCHSTRASSE 25
D-80538 MÜNCHEN

VERANTWORTLICH FÜR
DEN HERAUSGEBER/
RESPONSIBLE FOR
PUBLICATION:
STEFAN BOGNER

KONZEPT/CONCEPT:
STEFAN BOGNER
THIERSCHSTRASSE 25
D-80538 MÜNCHEN
SB@CURVES-MAGAZIN.COM

DELIUS KLASING
CORPORATE PUBLISHING
SIEKERWALL 21
D-33602 BIELEFELD

REDAKTION/
EDITORIAL CONTENT:
STEFAN BOGNER
BEN WINTER

ART DIRECTION, LAYOUT,
FOTOS/ART DIRECTION,
LAYOUT, PHOTOS:
STEFAN BOGNER

MAKING OF PHOTOS:
PHILIPP HEITSCH

TEXT/TEXT: BEN WINTER
TEXT INTRO/TEXT INTRO:
BEN WINTER

MOTIVAUSARBEITUNG,
LITHOGRAPHIE, SATZ/
POST-PRODUCTION,
LITHOGRAPHY, SETTING:
MICHAEL DORN

KARTENMATERIAL/MAP
MATERIAL: MAIRDUMONT,
OSTFILDERN

ÜBERSETZUNG/TRANSLATION:
JAMES O'NEILL

PRODUKTIONSLEITUNG/
PRODUCTION MANAGEMENT:
AXEL GERBER

DRUCK/PRINT:
KUNST- UND WERBEDRUCK,
BAD OEYNHAUSEN

1. AUFLAGE/1ST EDITION:
ISBN: 978-3-667-12749-5

AUSGEZEICHNET MIT / AWARDED WITH
DDC GOLD – DEUTSCHER DESIGNER CLUB E.V. FÜR GUTE GESTALTUNG 2011 // IF COMMUNICATION DESIGN AWARD 2012 BEST OF CORPORATE PUBLISHING 2012 // ADC BRONZE 2011 // RED DOT BEST OF THE BEST & D&AD 2012 // NOMINIERT FÜR DEN DEUTSCHEN DESIGNPREIS 2015 // WINNER AUTOMOTIVE BRAND CONTEST 2016 // GOOD DESIGN AWARD 2014

CURVES AUSGABEN / OTHER ISSUES OF CURVES

PYRENÄEN
PYRENEES
Im Handel erhältlich/Available in stores

ÖSTERREICH
AUSTRIA
Im Handel erhältlich/Available in stores

SCHWEIZ
SWITZERLAND
Im Handel erhältlich/Available in stores

SCHOTTLAND
SCOTLAND
Im Handel erhältlich/Available in stores

FRANKREICH
FRANCE
Im Handel erhältlich/Available in stores

USA • KALIFORNIEN
USA • CALIFORNIA
Im Handel erhältlich/Available in stores

SIZILIEN
SICILY
Im Handel erhältlich/Available in stores

NORDITALIEN
NORTHERN ITALY
Im Handel erhältlich/Available in stores

OSTDEUTSCHLAND
EASTERN GERMANY
Im Handel erhältlich/Available in stores

DEUTSCHLAND/DÄNE.
GERMANY/DENMARK
Im Handel erhältlich/Available in stores

SPANIEN • MALLORCA
SPAIN • MALLORCA
Im Handel erhältlich/Available in stores

USA • COLORADO/UTAH
USA • COLORADO/UTAH
Im Handel erhältlich/Available in stores

THAILAND
THAILAND
Im Handel erhältlich/Available in stores

SÜDDEUTSCHLAND
SOUTHERN GERMANY
Im Handel erhältlich/Available in stores

PORTUGAL
PORTUGAL
Im Handel erhältlich/Available in stores

ISLAND
ICELAND
Im Handel erhältlich/Available in stores

MALAYSIA
MALAYSIA
Im Handel erhältlich/Available in stores

NORWEGEN
NORWAY
Im Handel erhältlich/Available in stores

PATAGONIEN
PATAGONIA
Im Handel erhältlich/Available in stores

PORSCHE
911 Carrera S